THE BUSH PILOTS

THE BUSH PILOTS

A PICTORIAL HISTORY OF A CANADIAN PHENOMENON

BY J.A. FOSTER

M&S

McClelland & Stewart, Inc.
The Canadian Publishers
481 University Avenue
Toronto M5G 2E9

Canadian Cataloguing in Publication Data
Foster, J.A.
The bush pilots
ISBN 0-7710-3245-5
1. Bush pilots - Canada - History. 2. Aeronautics - Canada - History. I. Title.
TL523.S68 1990   629.13'0971   C89-090598-3

Design: Annabelle Stanley
Printed and bound in Canada

Acknowledgement and thanks to the Public Archives of Canada, the National Aviation Museum, the Canadian Forces Photographic Unit, the Provincial Archives of Manitoba, the Provincial Archives of Alberta, the Winnipeg *Free Press*, the City of Edmonton Archives, the City of Calgary Archives, the Richardson Archives, Wardair, Welland Phipps, Richard deBlicquy, Bradley Air Services, CP Air, Stephan Wilkinson, Z.L. Leigh, the Canadian Airways Limited Archives and the invaluable research and material provided by Peter Foster and Michael Hartley, without whose generous assistance, invaluable cooperation and support this book could never have been assembled.

Contents

Introduction
7
Beginnings
9
First Pilots
13
Barnstormers
21
First Commercial Ventures
35
New Frontiers
69
Search and Rescue
81
The Coming of Age
95
Growing Pains
129
The Second World War
169
End of an Era
187
Epilogue
213
Index
217

Introduction

In the late summer of 1950 I decided to become a bush pilot. There was no sense of the romance of aviation in this decision. Simply put: I needed a job. I was nineteen years old, air-force trained with a total of 152 hours of flying time. I had two things going for me: boundless optimism about my ability to deal with any aviation situation in which I might find myself, and a new crisp leather folder from the Department of Transport on which was embossed in gold: COMMERCIAL PILOT LICENCE. Much later I discovered that the two were not necessarily synonymous. The Royal Canadian Air Force had taught me the mechanics of flying, but it was as a bush pilot that I discovered the joy.

In the nearly forty years that have passed since that summer of decision in Winnipeg I have amassed many thousands of hours in more than a hundred types of aircraft around the world — on wheels, skis and floats; piston and jet; single- and multi-engine, from graceful gliders and tiny Piper J3 Cub crop dusters to Douglas DC7Fs. Trust me — for the pure joy of flying there

is nothing to equal the life of a bush pilot. Crop dusting is initially exciting, but once mastered it soon becomes repetitious and boring. Airline captains swiftly discover that they are little more than highly paid uniformed tour guides totally subordinate to on-board electronics and whichever air traffic controller they happened to be assigned. Flight instructors are poorly paid, and the boredom is relieved occasionally by a few welcomed seconds of mind-boggling terror. Executive flying is not only boring but requires such a grasp of corporate intrigue in order to please company executives that most pin-striped captains I know retired early in frustration or with peptic ulcers.

Bush flying is different. Every flight is unique, and there is a magic in each of the flying seasons. During spring breakup, when the northern lake ice disintegrates in a roar of protest, across the country float planes are slipped into the cold, clear water to begin their long summer of work. Each trip has a purpose, a challenge to a pilot's flying skills. An overloaded aircraft in a lake too small for a necessary take-off; landing in a grey overcast almost too low for safe visual flying; charging home through blinding rains or snowstorms when fuel is low and head winds high; the heart-stopping thrill of spinning out of control on water-covered ice after landing on skis; the sense of helplessness when trying to turn a weather-cocking float plane out of the wind and hold it from tipping into the water; the soft powder whisper of skis when touching down on newly fallen snow. Then there are the terrible winds with their mind-numbing cold, the swarms of voracious blackflies and harpoon mosquitoes. Yet above all there is the unquenchable warmth of companionship with those who have shared that splendid isolation and discovery of our Canadian north. I think it is this feeling, engraved so indelibly in each human heart, that has brought us together through such vast distances to become a nation.

Space does not permit full justice and recognition to the many hundreds of flyers and prospectors who, over six decades, were responsible for the exploration, mapping, development, supplying and ultimately the opening of our north. The stories presented here are brief historical glimpses of a few dozen of these astonishing pioneers. Yet each in his or her own way is representative of many hundreds.

This book is a modest tribute to those incredibly courageous bush pilots who came and went long before my time, and to those who followed after I left the scene.

Previous page: The lagoon at Carcross, Yukon. Home base for the National Geographic Expedition to the Yukon, March 1935. Aircraft are a Fokker Universal and a Fairchild of Northern Airways Ltd. (Public Archives of Canada, C 57647)

Beginnings

Wilbur and Orville Wright were the aviation fountain from which, ultimately, all the rivers of aircraft development flowed. Expanding upon ideas originated by the great German glider enthusiast Otto Lilienthal, the Wrights built a flimsy powered aircraft. Their fifty-seven-second achievement at Kitty Hawk, North Carolina, on 17 December, 1903, marked the beginning of powered flight by man.

The first Canadian aviation pioneers were three brothers on a homestead farm in Botha, Alberta. John, George and Elmer Underwood inherited a compulsion for tinkering from their father, John, who had invented the first disc plough. They knew little about the laws of aerodynamics, but as children they had built and flown a variety of kites. They drew up plans for their first flying machine around their kitchen table in the winter of 1906. The result looked nothing like any other early aircraft: a cut-out circle of canvas stretched across a frame and centred by a mast with an upright half circle of the same canvas. To transport the machine, the canvas was furled like a sail.

Directors of the Stettler Exhibition heard of the Underwood machine and asked the brothers to display it at their annual fair in the summer of 1907. The Toronto *Globe* reported: "It looked like a balloon with a huge gas bag." An enthusiastic Winnipeg reporter wrote that the machine had a five-hundred-horsepower motor. The first night of the exhibition the Underwoods sent the tethered machine aloft with a lantern swinging beneath its undercarriage. Next day, when the wind died, the brothers towed the four-hundred-pound contraption behind a team of galloping horses until it became airborne.

After the fair they built a graded landing strip near their farm and installed a small motor that allowed the awkward behemoth to taxi on its motorcycle wheels to the take-off position; then the motor was removed and the saucer kite was sent into the air. That summer the Underwoods experimented: a rudimentary rudder and ailerons were developed, and they demonstrated the machine's potential as a cargo carrier by loading it with five sacks of wheat. They towed it into the air, where it remained for a quarter of an hour. For a second flight, the sacks were unloaded, and John Underwood climbed aboard. Clinging to the struts on a short tether rope, he hovered happily thirty feet in the air for ten minutes. The next obvious step in the development of their machine was powered flight. They asked Glenn Curtiss in Hammondsport, New York, for a lightweight motorcycle engine. The price, $1,300, was too much for their resources, and reluctantly they abandoned further development.

A year later another Albertan, Reginald Hunt, from Edmonton, designed and built a craft with the wings of a box kite. It was powered with a gasoline engine. Hunt selected a hill overlooking the South Saskatchewan River to test his new machine. After a few successful flights he crashed. Disheartened, he gave up his experiments.

Meanwhile, on the other side of the country, in Baddeck, Nova Scotia, Glenn Curtiss had joined the Aerial Experimental Association (AEA), a group chaired by Alexander Graham Bell and his wife, Mabel. With no shortage of development funds the association managed within a year to produce three manned flying machines in Hammondsport and Baddeck. *Silver Dart,* the last of three AEA designs, was equipped with a new powerful water-cooled Curtiss motor. Bell arranged to bring *Silver Dart* to Baddeck for flight testing. There, on 23 February, 1909, with men on skates to steady its wings, J.A.D. McCurdy lifted *Silver Dart* from the ice of the Bras d'Or lake in front of Bell's summer home to deliver Canada into the aviation era. McCurdy flew *Silver Dart* a distance of half a mile while delighted townspeople looked on. It was the first flight by a British subject in a powered heavier-than-air machine in the British Empire.

Mabel Bell described the event in a letter to her daughter, Daisy: "Another perfect day, the *Silver Dart* made a short flight, coming down because the land was near. . . . We all pleaded with Papa for another flight but he was firm. It was the first flight of an airship in Canada and he would take no chances of disaster to spoil this first success." The next day McCurdy piloted *Silver Dart* on a circuitous flight that lasted six minutes.

The AEA disbanded in March 1909. The innovative ideas contributed by Bell and his associates formed the basis for all subsequent successful aircraft development. Curtiss returned to Hammondsport to begin commercial exploitation of ailerons, pontoons, tricycle-steerable undercarriages, airfoils, rudders and control surfaces. These, together with his engine designs, became the basis for the Curtiss Aircraft Company, and later the giant Curtiss-Wright Corporation.

Upon dissolution of the AEA, McCurdy and his friend Casey Baldwin, also an engineering graduate from the University of Toronto, organized the Canadian Aerodrome Company, with financial backing from the Bells, to manufacture aircraft at Baddeck. During the summer of 1909 they built three aircraft and shipped them by train to Camp Petawawa. In front of a group of sceptical military officers and government officials, they attempted to prove the poten-

tial of their airplanes as military weapons. Although *Silver Dart* made five separate flights of fifty miles per hour at fifty feet, McCurdy, blinded by the sun, clipped a sand dune on the fifth and demolished his fragile machine. The next day their second aircraft, *Baddeck No. 1*, crashed seventy yards after take-off. Canadian military officials concluded that airplanes were merely amusing toys with no practical military significance. Discouraged, McCurdy and Baldwin returned to Baddeck.

Despite setbacks aviation pioneers were thriving in western Canada. William Gibson, a prosperous young hardware merchant from Balgonie, Saskatchewan, developed a power plant for his kites out of the spring end of a window-blind roller. So successful was the design that he decided to build a large-scale engine. The plans were interrupted when he lost most of his fortune on a railroad-construction venture. He sold his chain of hardware stores and went prospecting for gold, with considerable success. Gibson sold his gold-producing properties for ten thousand dollars and moved to Victoria, British Columbia, where he set to work building his dream flying machine.

He experimented with a variety of kites from the cliffs outside Victoria. Residents scoffed at his efforts, flapping their arms at him in the street when he passed; but Gibson ignored them. He rented space at a local machine shop and built a six-cylinder aircraft engine to power his new flying machine. Equipped with two propellers and a four-wheel undercarriage, the awkward-looking *Gibson Twin* aircraft made its first flight early in 1910. It managed to remain airborne for two hundred feet before crashing into the trees. Gibson was thrown clear.

Elated by his success Gibson designed and built a second aircraft, *Gibson Multi-plane*, constructed of thin strips of spruce. (It was nicknamed "the venetian blind" by the locals.) For flight testing, Gibson moved the new machine to Calgary, where the weather was drier. After several successful flights the machine was destroyed when pilot Alex Japp tried to land in a field pitted with badger holes. Gibson, close to bankruptcy, gave up his aviation dreams and moved to San Francisco, where he turned his considerable inventive talents to the design and manufacturing of mining machinery.

The original Silver Dart in flight. (Public Archives of Canada, RE 64-2262)

First Pilots

In the summer of 1910, Walter Gilbert, a teenager from Cardwell, Ontario, attended Canada's first Aviation Meet at Lakeside, near Montreal. The event made a lasting impression on the young man. The grandstands were packed with spectators watching in astonishment as a variety of flimsy aircraft performed breath-taking stunts aloft. Count Jacques de Lesseps, grandson of the builder of the Suez Canal, set a new record for sustained flight in a Bleriot flying machine. A half century later Gilbert remembered that "the sight of those Demoiselles and Antoinettes took my breath away." Bitten by the aviation bug, he was determined to become a pilot.

When war broke out in Europe, Gilbert joined the army as a junior inspector of shrapnel with the Imperial Munitions Board. Later, when a British Recruiting Mission opened an office for the Royal Flying Corps (RFC), Gilbert applied. "I had no concrete idea what the corps was all about, except that it was one way to get to war." After initial flying training in Toronto, Ontario, with the RFC's first flying instructors, who had only a few more hours' experience in the air than their students, Gilbert was shipped off to England. He took an advanced training course that included gunnery instruction at the RFC's Central Flying School in Uphavon and upon graduation was ordered to France. At the time the average life expectancy for new pilots at the front was three to six weeks. Locked in deadly combat over the trenches with the more experienced German pilots, the RFC greenhorns learned swiftly how to fight and fly - or they died. Gilbert was one of the lucky ones.

The young flyers of the First World War, who would become Canada's bush pilots, came from a range of economic and cultural backgrounds. Donald MacLaren, one of Canada's leading aces, had no burning desire to fly. He signed with the Royal Flying Corps in Toronto in 1917 so he could visit his girl-friend.

Norman Forrester was a boxer who wanted to become a doctor but after seeing an exciting recruiting poster, he left the medical corps in France and signed up for flying training.

Carl Falkenberg was recovering in a Scottish hospital from shell shock after a night artillery attack on Vimy Ridge when he noticed an RFC advertisement in the *London Mail*. To avoid being sent back to the trenches, he enlisted in the air force.

Seventeen-year-old Clennell Haggerston ("Punch") Dickins went to France with a battalion from the University of Alberta. A few days in the trenches convinced him that his military career opportunities lay elsewhere. He applied immediately for transfer to the RFC.

Bertie Hollick-Kenyon served overseas with the British Columbia Horse. He was wounded in the trenches, judged unfit for further military service and discharged. Instead of going home, he joined the RFC.

Wilfrid May saw a photograph in the *Illustrated London News* of Allied planes strafing German trenches. The idea of flying to war instead of standing in the mud was most appealing. After a year and a half in the 202nd infantry battalion, during which he rose to sergeant machine-gunner in France, May was posted to the RFC in England. As a student he flew a French-built Caudron fighter with a rotary engine and warpable bamboo wings instead of ailerons.

He learned to his surprise that he had that unique combination of timing, judgement, visual perception, aircraft feel and self-confidence that marks a natural pilot, and soon discovered that he had a charmed life where aircraft were concerned. On a trip in a Bristol fighter with an observer to Northholt Airport, an R.E. 8 reconnaissance aircraft landed on top of May's plane. No one received a scratch from the incident. Ordered back to Northholt to pick up a Sopwith Camel, May watched in horror as the aircraft he was to collect landed on his instructor and blew up. Still in one piece, May shipped out to France.

The French air base at St. Omar, just west of the Belgian border, served as a pilots' pool for replacements at the front. Pilots flew reconnaissance patrols until their orders arrived. There were a number of Canadians at St. Omar when May arrived. George Gorman and Conway Farrell were the first to greet him. The under-age Farrell had joined the 128th Moose Jaw Battalion before transferring into the RFC. Gorman had completed his initial flying training at Camp Borden, Ontario, after which he had been assigned to train Canadian pilots at Fort Worth, Texas.

There were other Canadians at St. Omar. Fred McCall had arrived in England with the Canadian Expeditionary Force. After a winter of ankle-deep mud on the Salisbury Plain he transferred to the RFC where he was commissioned as a lieutenant. Harold Oaks enlisted in the Canadian Corps of Signals and had already seen active service in France as a dispatch rider. He thought an airplane would be more exciting to drive than a motor bike and switched to the RFC. Jimmy Bell learned to fly an open-front French-designed Farman, nicknamed "the rumpety" because of the noise its wheels made bumping along the turf during take-

off. A slow, ungainly biplane with short, stubby landing skids, the overweight Farman had a seventy-horsepower motor that could manage to lift the aircraft to three thousand feet only on a cool day.

It required courage to fly these early machines in combat. There were no parachutes issued. The aircraft had no brakes. The pilot sat on a wicker seat over the fuel tank. A single incendiary bullet in the right place would turn the machine into a flaming coffin. A pilot had the choice of burning alive on the way down, jumping from the cockpit to certain death or using his service revolver to shoot himself.

There were many aircraft accidents on the ground and in the air, particularly during flying training. Leigh Brintnell was standing with a group of his student pilots at a training base in England as a trainee did aerobatics. They watched in horror as the pilot made a low inverted pass — too low. As the machine roared across the field, the pilot's head was scraped off. The aircraft crumpled into a ball of twisted fabric, wood and metal. Calmly, Brintnell strode across the field to another trainer, took off and successfully executed the same manoeuvre.

The single-seat Sopwith Camel with its twin Vickers machine-guns was the foremost fighter aircraft in the RFC. Designed by Thomas Murdoch Sopwith, whose company also designed the Snipe, the Camel got its name because of the fairing hump covering its machine-guns. It was an unstable, tail-heavy machine and a menace to fly in inexperienced hands. Yet Allied pilots shot down more enemy aircraft with the Camel than with all other planes produced in the First World War.

By the end of hostilities one third of the pilots in the RFC were Canadians. The war in the air produced its roster of heroes on both sides. Flight Lieutenant Edward Grange became Canada's first flying "ace" in January 1917. During a four-day period his guns brought down five German aircraft.

Opposite page: Lieutenant Wilfrid (Wop) May, Royal Flying Corps, at the Front, First World War. (Private Collection)

Wounded in action, he was awarded the Distinguished Service Cross. In spring of 1917 the RFC found itself critically short of aircraft and pilots. During "Bloody April," the RFC lost a staggering 40 per cent of its air crew to German guns despite its superiority in numbers. The effect on the survivors who faced the growing numbers of empty chairs in the officers' mess at mealtimes can be imagined. A decision was made to transfer the Royal Naval Air Service (RNAS) to bolster the thinning numbers of RFC men and machines along the Western Front. Most famous among the Canadian RNAS pilots was Raymond Collishaw, who commanded a flight in 10 Squadron. Between May and July 1917, Collishaw's group of five Canadians claimed eighty-seven victories — thirty-three of them by Collishaw.

The abilities of the German pilots are best illustrated by RFC losses after the Battle of the Somme: 800 RFC aircraft destroyed with a loss of 252 pilots against German losses of 359 aircraft and 43 dead. Although British senior military officers considered Canadian pilots to be semi-trained, the Canadian pilots produced the lion's share of victories in the air. The Canadians' superiority lay in Canadian training methods.

At the top of the Allied list was William Avery Bishop, the Royal Military College drop-out, with seventy-two German aircraft to his credit — twenty-five of them in a Nieuport fighter during his last twelve days at the front. Bishop's record earned him the Victoria Cross (VC), Military Cross (MC), the Distinguished Service Order (DSO) twice and the Distinguished Flying Cross (DFC).

Although the twenty-two-year-old Bishop was only an average pilot, he turned himself into a superb marksman in the air. He had set the convergence point of the Lewis guns in his Nieuport at one hundred yards. Few pilots had the skill or courage to hold their fire until they brought their aircraft this close to the enemy. At one hundred yards it was difficult for Bishop to miss his opponent.

Bishop trained initially as an observer for artillery-spotting duties. He completed his first tour of duty at the front and was invalided to England with a minor wound. He re-mustered as a pilot and after training returned to the front. Upon hearing that some pilots had experienced the loss of their testicles from ground fire, Bishop flew into combat sitting on an iron frying pan stolen from the cookhouse.

Seventy years later much controversy would be raised about the accuracy of Bishop's count of seventy-two victories. Keeping records of a pilot's score in France was always difficult. Although the word "victory" was translated into "destruction" by generals, politicians and newspaper reporters, the pilots did not see things in the same light. In the fury of smoke, weather and ground fire, pilots often did not see their opponents crash. "Victories" in their reports were given different classifications: down out of control; driven down; forced to land; crashed; on fire. Questionable victories were sometimes confirmed by other pilots or ground troops. Bishop's record in 1918 was fifty-one authenticated kills, twenty-five down out of control, three driven down, three forced to land and three artillery spotting balloons. He had more authenticated victories than any other Allied flyer.

On the German side of the lines, Baron Manfred von Richthofen held the wartime record with eighty aircraft shot down in twenty months. In 1917 he had been awarded Germany's highest decoration, Pour la Mérite, or Blue Max, as it was nicknamed. Richthofen was twenty-five when he took over command of the "circus" (squadron), and he had already written his memoirs. Most of his kills — as with most of the top scoring aces — were slow-moving reconnaissance aircraft; apart from one Belgian Spad, his victims were all British. Canadian Captain A. Roy Brown was given credit for the Red Baron's defeat.

On Sunday morning, 21 April, 1918, both men were suffering from what later came to be understood as extreme battle fatigue from their months of constant aerial combat. Brown's squadron, located at Bertangles, was only twenty miles from Richthofen's base at Cappy. Brown, a combat veteran, had eleven victories to his credit. Prior to being posted to France, he had served with the RNAS patrolling the Belgian coast and providing fighter cover for Allied bombers flying into Germany. Skies were overcast with a threat of rain when Brown's flight of Sopwith Camels took off from Bertangles, their Clerget motors barking in the crisp morning air. Wilfrid May, who had just arrived from the pilot pool at St. Omar, was on his first combat mission. Brown ordered him to stay at the periphery of any action and watch how the experienced pilots handled their machines.

Behind the German lines, Richthofen's Staffel II, comprising three five-plane formations, lifted off at 10:30 A.M. Shortly after, Brown's planes were airborne in the British sector. The Baron was ten days short of his twenty-sixth birthday. The squadrons met over the front. Seeing that he outnumbered the Allied aircraft Richthofen gave the signal to attack. Richthofen preferred to stay high above every dogfight, where he would wait for a "cripple" who broke for home, then drop down for an easy kill. This morning his target was greenhorn Lieutenant Wilfrid ("Wop") May.

Following Brown's orders, May observed the air battle from a safe distance over the German lines as Spandau and Vickers machine-guns clattered above the road between St. Hamel and Sailly-le-Sec. A Fokker triplane with blue camouflage passed beneath him. Ignoring orders, May dived to the attack, firing as the Camel passed below his opponent. He saw the German pilot slump in his seat, then the Fokker fell away in a spiral towards the ground. May soared into a vertical turn and began firing at other

Fokkers until the heat from his guns caused them to jam. In frustration, he spun down from the fight and headed for the British lines.

On the way home he caught sight of a red Fokker triplane diving on his tail from out of the sun. Richthofen's twin Spandaus aimed for an easy kill. May banged open his throttle and began to twist and turn in an attempt to break loose from the German's line of fire. It was no use. The Baron kept closing the distance between them. May dived for the Somme. Richthofen followed, something that normally he would never have done. The two aircraft roared over the German and British trenches where troops opened up on pursuer and pursued. Bullet holes appeared through the wing fabric of both aircraft. May hugged the ground. The gap between the two aircraft narrowed to no more than seventy-five feet. Expecting the *coup de grâce* within moments, May turned in his seat to see a Camel diving behind the red Fokker.

Roy Brown had seen the irrepressible May spin out of the battle, and he had noticed the red Fokker following him. It was unusual for Richthofen to cross the lines into British airspace, but so intent was he on his easy kill that he forgot to look behind him. The moment he was within range, Brown fired. He saw Richthofen straighten for an instant in the seat then fall forward against the instrument panel. The Fokker did a short half spin then crashed alongside a trench in the Australian sector of the line. Richthofen's broken body was found strapped in the cockpit, still holding the joystick. The corpse was removed and carried on a sheet of corrugated iron to a hangar at Bertangles.

It was discovered that the Baron had died instantaneously from a single bullet through the heart. Later, the Australians would claim their ground fire had brought Richthofen down, but the angle at which the bullet entered the body proved that it came from above the red Fokker. Brown was given the credit. Carl Falkenberg saw the crash crew bring in the body and the wrecked triplane. Little remained of the aircraft. Pilots ripped off every bit of fabric for good luck, while mechanics dismantled the Baron's Spandau guns. Later, Falkenberg recalled with wonder: "Richthofen was only a small fair-haired man with a frail delicate face. He certainly did not look like the legendary figure who had killed so many of our pilots."

The British arranged a full military funeral with honours for their fallen foe. Six pilots from the newly formed Royal Air Force (RAF) carried the black-stained wooden casket to an open grave near a lone poplar tree in the Bertangles cemetery. An Anglican chaplain read the burial service. Allied officers lined up to salute the open grave. A volley of rifle fire by an Australian detachment provided the final salute. Falkenberg and his fellow pilots placed a broken four-blade propeller as a headstone. A few days later, over German lines, the RAF dropped a cannister containing a photograph of the grave and its wreaths. In an odd way the courageous Richthofen had become a hero to the Allies. Herman Göring took over command of the Richthofen Flying Circus for the five remaining months of the war. (In 1936, when the Edmonton Grads basketball team went to Germany to compete in the Berlin Olympics, they took with them May's fragment of the red Fokker. It was presented as a gesture of friendship to Baroness von Richthofen, the German ace's elderly mother.)

After fourteen months at the front, Roy Brown, the giant-killer, had the lined and haggard face of an old man. He was invalided out to England with bleeding ulcers. As the war wound down, there were other casualties among the Canadian pilots. Walter Gilbert nearly died from the Spanish influenza, which in two years wiped out more people on both sides of the front lines than were killed in battle casualties. Don MacLaren was grounded with a broken leg after a wrestling match with a junior officer. During eight months, MacLaren had shot down forty-eight German aircraft and six balloons, and he rose to command his squadron.

By coincidence, his first dogfight, early in 1918, took place on the same day and at the same time that American Captain Eddie Rickenbacker was engaged in his first battle. Rickenbacker went on to became America's top scorer (with twenty-one aircraft), a national hero and Congressional Medal of Honor winner.

During one sortie, Fred McCall's friend Brooke Claxton was wounded and crashed behind enemy lines. McCall returned safely to base, while Claxton, who became Canada's Minister of National Defence after the Second World War, spent the rest of the conflict in a German military hospital. Anti-aircraft fire brought Lieutenant George Gorman down behind German lines. He spent the war's closing months in a German prison camp.

Wop May's mild manners on the ground contradicted his exuberance in the air, where he destroyed thirteen aircraft and earned a reputation as an awesome stunt pilot. While strafing enemy troops during the Battle of Amiens, May was shot in the face and arms by flak. Somehow he managed to bring his bullet-riddled Camel home and land it safely.

There were a few malingerers. When the undercarriage of a plane in Falkenberg's squadron clipped the top off a four-holer latrine, the quartet of men inside claimed that they had suffered severe shock and promptly put in for sick leave.

When the war ended, Billy Bishop led the Canadian, British and American scorers with seventy-two kills. Ray Collishaw was third with sixty; D.R. MacLaren had fifty-four; W.G. Barker claimed fifty-three; McCall and Claxton had thirty-seven each; and Cy

Becker's tally was eighteen. With the airmen who had kept their machines repaired and flying, they packed their kits and duffel bags and boarded the ships that would take them home. For some it was a relief to be returning to the life that they had left behind — jobs, sweethearts or wives and children. For the younger ones, those who had worked at no other job but war, the party was finally over.

Barnstormers

"The tragedy of war is that it must end," observed an astute eighteen-year-old Swedish King Charles XII after crushing the Danes in 1700, then forcing them to accept a humiliating peace.

Those Canadian airmen who had revelled in the comradeship and excitement of wartime action were welcomed home as heroes, then quickly dismissed from the service as part of their government's post-war austerity measures. The "war to end all wars" had been too costly to contemplate the expense of employing idle pilots and their ground crews. Politicians of every stripe were convinced that in this new enlightened age wars were a thing of the past. So what purpose was there in maintaining an air force?

The public began to lose interest in aviation and its wartime heroes. People associated flying with deeds of daring, violence and an early death. The government sold its surplus wartime aircraft at bargain-basement prices. Twelve hundred dollars would buy a Curtiss JN-4 Canuck "Jenny" trainer in first-class condition. A number of ex-air force pilots scrounged the money to buy themselves a piece of the past, only to discover that civilian airfields for handling aircraft were few and far between. The pilots knew little about maintenance so there were accidents across the country. Every small airfield soon had its bone-yard of wrecked and rusting aircraft. Most pilots gave up their dream machines and found honest employment. Wop May was one of the few exceptions.

Captain Wilfred May, DFC, returned

First airmail to Edmonton. (l to r) Katherine Stinson, Bill Stark and Postmaster George Armstrong. American Katherine Stinson, the flying schoolgirl from Missouri, was one of the greatest of pre-war pilots. She became the first woman to loop-the-loop and later inaugurated the idea of sky-writing. Her aerobatic display at the Calgary Stampede of 1916 dazzled spectators. She volunteered to fight as a pilot in the Royal Flying Corps but was politely turned down; thereupon she became an ambulance driver overseas. (City of Edmonton Archives, A81-26)

Jenny aircraft, *City of Edmonton*, Wop May's first commercial aircraft operation. (Public Archives of Canada, C57589)

home to Edmonton in 1919 a hero with a yearning to continue doing what he knew he did best. He had little money and no prospects. Then the gods smiled. A Curtiss JN-4 was offered to the city of Edmonton by a Montreal business tycoon who had made a bundle in Edmonton real estate and decided to repay the city for its largesse. After a brief discussion, Mayor Joe Clarke and the city council accepted the gift and named the aircraft after the city. Sensing an opportunity to fly again, May asked if he could rent the plane. The council agreed. A price of twenty-five dollars per month was established, and Wop agreed to maintain the machine and promote flying in Edmonton (a "dry lease" in today's aviation terminology). With the necessary paperwork completed, Wop and his brother Court raised the required capital and formed May Airplanes Ltd. Ex-RFC flyer George Gorman, released from a German prison camp after the war, joined the venture, with Peter Derbyshire as mechanic. It was the first

commercial bush operation in Canada.

The May brothers hauled their aircraft by car to Walter Sproule's pasture, just inside the city limits, which became Edmonton's first airport. "We built a crude hangar for servicing the Jenny then announced optimistically that we were open and ready for business," Wop explained.

But there wasn't much business. Gorman and May performed aerobatics at local fairs, and the usual crowd of wide-eyed youngsters without money wanted rides after the show. In Edmonton, during the western part of his Canadian tour, H.R.H. Edward, Prince of Wales, was treated to a spectacular display of aerobatics by Wop, for no fee. But the company needed steady work to remain in business, to provide a worthwhile service at a profit.

May approached the publisher of the

Edmonton Journal with a proposition to carry the noon edition of his paper each day by air to the town of Wetaskiwin, sixty-five miles south of the city. The publisher decided to give the service a try. Next day, Gorman and Derbyshire loaded the newspapers plus two canvas sacks of advertising circulars and took off for Wetaskiwin following the rail line. Gorman flew at five hundred feet with Derbyshire in the front seat flinging leaflets announcing their new service over each community along the way. Over Wetaskiwin, Gorman circled the race track, where the newspaper's representative was standing, waving his arms. Gorman brought the Jenny down to twenty feet above the ground, and Derbyshire tossed out the bags. On the way home they ran into heavy rain and turbulence and were forced down in a muddy field. (They barely missed a cemetery on their approach.) When the wind dropped, Gorman took off and returned to Edmonton, completing the first commercial flight in western Canada.

Not to be outdone, the rival *Bulletin*, Edmonton's oldest newspaper, hired Gorman to drop free copies of its publication on two thousand picnickers at a meeting of the United Farmers of Alberta in the town of St. Albert. The excitement broke up the meeting.

To promote the company, Wop went on a western tour of rodeos and country fairs where he gave exhibitions of wing-walking, aerobatics and parachute-jumping while Gorman and Derbyshire gave plane rides at twenty dollars per person for three minutes aloft. (This is about seventy-five dollars a minute in today's dollars.) All across the North American continent ex-air force pilots and mechanics in clapped-out war-surplus aircraft were looking for work. Men and aircraft crisscrossed the country

Captain Wilfrid (Wop) May, DFC, at the Calgary Exhibition, 1919 (Provincial Archives of Alberta, 68.78/12)

Sunday afternoon crowd gathers to wave as Wop May lands at Edmonton's first airport on the farm of Walter Sproule at the edge of the city, 1920. (Provincial Archives of Alberta, 13)

visiting every likely-looking town or village in a search for passengers. Any level field served as an airstrip. People came from miles around to gawk and, if they could afford it, go up for a three-minute ride.

Short of money, the airmen used local barns for sleeping quarters and temporary maintenance hangars. The word "barn-storming" entered the vocabulary. If business was slow, a pilot might put on a low-level aerobatic show to stir a little excitement. As the stunts became more spectacular, there were accidents. Regulations were needed to ensure public safety. A federal Air Board came into being in 1919, to control all military and civil aviation in Canada.

That was a year of aviation firsts in Canada. The first official airmail flew between Canada and the United States when Eddie Hubbard, with William Boeing, piloted a Boeing C3 seaplane between Vancouver and Seattle on March 3. Four months later John Alcock and Arthur Brown made

the first direct transatlantic flight in a Vickers Vimy biplane from St. John's, Newfoundland, to Clifden, Ireland. The fact that the aircraft ended up on its nose in a bog was irrelevant. In July, Frank Ellis made the first parachute jump by a Canadian in Canada from a Curtiss JN-4 biplane at Crystal Beach, Ontario. In Parrsboro, Nova Scotia, Majors Brackley and Gwan made the nation's first multi-passenger flight in a Handley-Page bomber with fourteen people on board. Over on the west coast, Ernest Hoy flew the first aircraft across the Rockies from Vancouver to Calgary via Lethbridge.

Hoy's flight was sponsored by two Alberta newspapers. Hoy, a twenty-four-year-old RFC veteran, was selected in a draw by

George Gorman (on right, above; on left, below) loads copies of the *Edmonton Journal* for air delivery to Wetaskiwin, 60 miles south of the city, 1919. (above: City of Edmonton Archives, a81-26; below: Public Archives of Canada, C 57728)

CAPT. F.R. McCALL. DSO-M.C.&-BAR-D.FC.
CALGARY EXHIBITION-1919.
PHOTO-OLIVER.

Above: Captain Fred R. McCall DSO, MC & Bar, DFC. Calgary Exhibition, 1919. (Public Archives of Canada, C 59781)

Left: Fred McCall in his Curtiss Jenny, 1929. (Public Archives of Canada, C 43976)

members of the Vancouver Aerial League of Canada to make the flight. On 7 August, 1919, he took off in a Curtiss Jenny from Minoru Park on Lulu Island near Vancouver with an extra fuel tank strapped in the aircraft's front seat. Unable to climb above seven thousand feet, Hoy flew between mountain peaks, squeaking through the Crawford Pass one hundred and fifty feet above the rocky crags. Buffeted by vicious drafts and air currents that drove his Jenny up and down hundreds of feet at a time, Hoy had great difficulty in controlling the aircraft, which was already nose-heavy because of the extra fuel tank. At Lethbridge he refueled and headed to Calgary. Gasoline flares and the headlights from hundreds of spectators' cars lit up Bowness Park for Hoy's arrival. He touched down safely an hour after sunset.

On his return flight, just after take-off at Golden, British Columbia, Hoy banked sharply to avoid hitting two boys on the runway. Near the end of the field he banked again to avoid a huge cottonwood tree. His left wing clipped the ground and the Jenny cartwheeled in a shower of sand and gravel. Badly shaken, Hoy returned to Vancouver by rail and gave up flying. Later he settled in Georgia.

While Gorman and Derbyshire were busy working the exhibition circuit, veteran Fred McCall staged an aerial display at the Calgary Stampede. In the vernacular of the time, it turned out to be "a humdinger."

McCall took off from the exhibition's race-track with the manager's two young sons. At 250 feet his engine quit. Faced with a choice of returning to the race track, where a competition was under way, or landing in the midway, McCall chose the midway. He brought the Jenny down and stalled it directly over the merry-go-round, where it dropped with a crunch on the roof, its engine wedged firmly by the centre pole. Fortunately, no one was hurt. The enterprising midway manager promptly opened a booth and began selling tickets to view the spectacle, splitting the profits with McCall. So successful was the new exhibit that McCall lugged the damaged machine to Edmonton the following week to put in the city's Big Victory Fair. As an added attraction he hired a wing walker and a very nervous novice parachutist. McCall advised the jumper not to worry, as in his experience "parachutes always opened nine times out of ten." Taking McCall at his word, the man made nine jumps then quit.

In the summer of 1919, for a big baseball game at Edmonton's Renfrew Park between the Edmonton Veterans and the Calgary Hustlers, Wop May was hired to give an aerobatic performance in his Jenny, now called the *Edmonton*. Then he would make a low pass across the field so that Mayor Clarke, who was riding as a passenger, could throw out the first ball. Clarke, who had never flown and who had no wish to try, was finally persuaded for the sake of the city's honour. At game time Wop and the mayor took off and circled the field, where both teams were lined up and waiting. For twenty minutes May went through his stunning aerobatic display, culminating in a low pass across home plate and a vertical roll into the sky. The ashen-faced Clarke, ill and shivering with fright, forgot to throw the ball. Annoyed, May insisted that they return to home plate. On the second pass, at ten feet in the air, Clarke threw the ball, which was caught by the catcher to the cheers of the crowd. The game got under way. Wop landed, helped the mayor from his seat and inquired how His Honour had enjoyed the trip. Swaying unsteadily on rubbery legs, Clarke announced to reporters that in his opinion Wop May was crazy as a hoot owl, and that he would never go up in an airplane again.

In the east, the two Victoria Cross winners, Billy Bishop and William G. Barker, optimistically formed the Bishop-Barker Flying Company to fly weekend passengers

When Fred McCall made an emergency landing on a carousel at the Calgary Stampede Exhibition grounds, the enterprising midway manager promptly set up a booth and charged admission for a peek at the shattered Jenny pinned to the top of the merry-go-round. (Public Archives of Canada, C 57765)

from Toronto to the Muskoka Lakes holiday area. In the days before fast cars and passable roads, the only practical way to travel to Muskoka was by rail. Bishop and Barker speculated enthusiastically that this regular summer weekend travel could be changed from a lengthy, boring train ride to a brief, pleasurable trip by air. Unfortunately, the regular Muskoka travellers did not share their enthusiasm, and the Bishop-Barker venture went out of business.

Wartime aerial photographic reconnaissance had proved invaluable for analyzing enemy positions and intentions; photographs of the Western Front had been updated daily. In 1919 the same principle was applied to commercial use in Canada's first aerial survey. The H.V. Greene Aerial Survey Company Limited was formed to carry an expedition to Labrador. Two former US Navy

pilots took some fifteen thousand photographs of timberland.

May and Gorman formed a partnership, the May-Gorman Company, and expanded their activities into the freight and aerial photography business. They flew into the Peace River country northeast of Edmonton. There were no maps. Navigation was done strictly by visual contact with the ground, by compass, by guess and by God. North of the fiftieth parallel, the angle of declination by a compass needle made accurate navigation nearly impossible. When he went to Peace River, May took surveyor George MacLeod along as navigator, because MacLeod knew the country. On the return trip they were forced down in a bush clearing with engine trouble and had to walk to the town of Athabasca for help. In due course Derbyshire arrived and repaired the

Above: Wop May circles Edmonton's Renfrew Ball Park while players wait expectantly for Mayor Joe Clarke to throw out the first ball of the season from the aircraft's cockpit. The city's Brewing and Malting Company is in the background, 1920. (City of Edmonton Archives, A81-26)

Right: FLY FLY FLY. (City of Edmonton Archives)

Previous page: Wop May flies over the Tegler Building in downtown Edmonton, 1920. (Public Archives of Canada, C 57726)

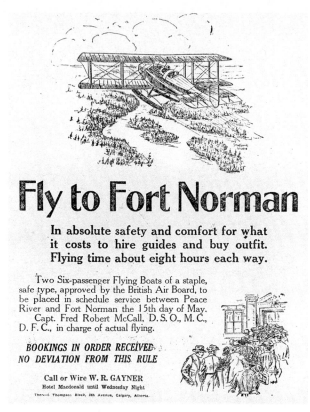

FLY TO FORT NORMAN. (City of Edmonton Archives)

Jenny for the flight to Edmonton. Next, May and Gorman looked to Saskatchewan in search of business. They flew cargo, gave rides at country fairs, barnstormed and picked up whatever was available to turn a dollar.

Meanwhile, in Quebec, the Laurentide Company, a pulp and paper manufacturer, arranged to borrow two Curtiss HS-2L flyingboats from the Air Board to carry out a survey in the St. Maurice River valley. The timber owners and operators in the area formed the St. Maurice Forestry Protective Association. Stuart Graham, a former RNAS pilot, flew the machines from Dartmouth, Nova Scotia, to the base of operations at Lac la Tortue. In addition to aerial photography and sketching timber limits, the aircraft were used for personnel transport and forest-fire patrols. Eventually, the directors of Laurentide decided they would prefer to purchase flying time rather than operate their own aircraft, and in 1922 Laurentide Air Service Ltd. was formed to provide that service.

Private pilot's licence No. 1 was issued on 24 January, 1920, to Stanley Scott of Ottawa. Three months later in Regina, Robert McCombie received air engineer certificate No. 1. On the same day, in Regina, a Curtiss JN-4 owned by the Aerial Service Company Ltd. donned the lettering G-CAAA and became the country's first commercially registered aircraft.

Hard on the heels of these bureaucratic developments, on 30 June, 1920, came provisional approval to establish a Canadian air force composed of 1,340 officers and

3,905 enlisted men. Equipped with an assortment of Felixstowe F.3, Curtiss H-16 and Naval Air Service HS-2L flying-boats, the new air force spent the bulk of its flying time in a variety of civil activities for various provincial governments.

Aviation's post-war boom peaked in 1920. Then the novelty of heroic pilots and their aircraft began to wear thin. The brief era of the barnstormers was over. People who had wanted to experience the thrill of flying had taken their trips. Except in specialized situations, flying could not be commercially justified. The nation slid into one of its periodic financial recessions. As business dried up and aircraft motors wore out,

most of the pilots, older and wiser, drifted into less hazardous occupations, married and settled down.

Fred McCall's company went bankrupt, along with several others. McCall gave up flying temporarily and became a liquor salesman in Calgary. For several years, with the exception of Laurentide Pulp and Paper, Canadian commercial aviation wallowed quietly in the doldrums.

Fairey Mark IIIC seaplane of the Canadian Air Board prior to first trans-Canada flight in October 1920. (Public Archives of Canada, C 43012)

First Commercial Ventures

In the summer of 1920 an Imperial Oil Limited geologist, Theodore Link, reported finding oil on Bear Island in the Mackenzie River fifty miles down river from the trapping community of Fort Norman in the Northwest Territories. The news came as no surprise to people living in the area. Passengers travelling on the Hudson's Bay Company's stern-wheelers had noticed oil slicks on the Mackenzie River for years. News of the Black Gold strike stirred some excitement in the cities to the south. As winter approached, numbers of prospectors headed for the strike area by dog team. Since the area lay more than eight hundred miles north of the nearest railway, the Royal Canadian Mounted Police tried to discourage amateur adventurers who knew little or nothing about sub-Arctic winter survival. The RCMP wanted no repetition of the hundreds who died trying to reach the Klondike gold fields only twenty-five years earlier.

Charles Taylor, Imperial Oil's representative in Edmonton, realized that the find was too far north for existing commercial production. However, he felt that the oil properties should be added to the company's general reserves. Once spring breakup arrived, Taylor knew, the area would be alive with prospectors travelling by canoe and boat, staking out their claims. To get a head start on the army of anticipated prospectors Taylor persuaded Imperial Oil's Toronto head office to buy two aircraft and fly the necessary men and supplies into the discovery site long before spring breakup. The site lay only 850 miles north of Edmonton by air. (The journey was twice that distance overland.) Astutely, Imperial Oil's executives agreed to Taylor's proposal and quickly located two German-built Junkers single-engine cabin aircraft in New York. The aircraft were part of German war reparations.

Wop May and George Gorman were hired to fly them to Edmonton. In later years May would admit that if the Imperial Oil contract hadn't come when it did the May-Gorman Company would have folded. May, Gorman and Derbyshire left by train for New York in November. A few days after Christmas, they took off from the air base at Mineola, Long Island, to begin the long flight home. Flying together, the two Junkers touched down for fuel at Belfontaine, Sandusky, Cleveland, Chicago and Minneapolis before crossing the border and flying to Winnipeg. They flew blind without radios or weather information, using standard road maps and rulers to navigate. In Manitoba poor visibility and heavy icing conditions forced the Junkers down at Virden. When the weather cleared, Gorman's aircraft hit a fence on take-off damaging the tail. May left him behind to make repairs while he continued to Saskatoon, flying through patchy fog at six hundred feet. He had telegraphed his estimated time of arrival from Saskatoon.

A crowd gathered at the May-Gorman airport in anticipation of May's arrival. The reception committee built a bonfire to keep warm. As darkness fell on 6 January, 1921, May sighted the flaming beacon and landed. The temperature was -38°C. May switched off the motor, staggered out of the unheated aircraft and announced to the crowd: "Thank you all for coming. Now if you don't mind I think I'll sleep for about a week." Gorman and Derbyshire arrived a few days later.

The Fort Norman Expedition assembled for the trip north. Lieutenant Elmer Fullerton, an air force pilot on a leave of absence, and William Hill, a mechanic, were taken on the payroll. Dominion Land Surveyor William Waddell came along to stake Imperial Oil's claims. RCMP Sergeant Hubert (Nitchie) Thorne joined the expedition. Thorne was returning to his post at Fort Simpson after escorting Albert Lebeau, accused of murdering his wife, to Edmonton to stand trial. The eight-hour plane ride would save the Mountie a two-month trip by dog-sled.

The two Junkers, nicknamed *Rene* and *Vic*, set out on the first leg of their journey to Peace River, 275 miles northeast of Edmonton. The flyers carried sleeping bags, snowshoes, blow torches and emergency supplies for ten days. In Peace River, a small trapping community, the flyers set up a base camp. A hangar and living quarters had been prepared, and a rough airstrip cleared and levelled in preparation for the expedition's arrival. The aircraft were hoisted by cable and derrick and their wheels exchanged for skis. The base was only a short distance from where the great Scottish explorer and fur trader, Alexander Mackenzie, the first European in the area, had wintered in 1793 before starting out on his overland trip to the Pacific Ocean.

For the next leg a fuel cache was organized at the Hudson's Bay Company trading post at Upper Hay River. The Indians at Upper Hay River had never seen an aircraft. When the first Junkers landed on the river ice, a group of armed Indians appeared on the bank. They stood watching at a safe distance as the aircraft was unloaded. Despite Fullerton's smiles and waves, they could not be enticed closer. When the Junkers arrived in Peace River on the return trip, Fullerton noticed with astonishment

that there were a number of bullet holes in one of the aircraft's wings.

The plan was to refuel at Upper Hay River, then fly to Hay River on the southwest shore of Great Slave Lake. At the mid-point of their next leg the pilots flew into a severe winter storm and had to swing southeast and put down at Fort Vermilion for two days, waiting until the weather cleared. On the flight to Hay River in cloudless skies they took the first aerial photographs of the Northwest Territories' bleak and empty landscape.

Junkers Fl3 aircraft *Rene* of Imperial Oil Co. after crash landing at Fort Simpson, Northwest Territories, March 1921. (Public Archives of Canada, C 36414)

The next refuelling stop after Hay River was Fort Providence, where they landed on a small lake. Local Indians on snow-shoes were employed to tramp down the soft powdered snow so the aircraft could take off. It took three tries to get the aircraft into the air. Beyond Fort Providence the expedition was plagued by a succession of near disasters. They had planned to land on the Mackenzie River at Fort Simpson but found the ice had frozen into a rough washboard with dangerous rifts. The Junkers circled the settlement, searching for a smooth landing site. Gorman tried a landing first with *Rene*, but on touchdown his skis hit a deeply rutted dog-sled track hidden beneath the snow. The aircraft nosed over, its propeller and undercarriage badly damaged. Fortunately, Fullerton managed to land *Vic* close by without mishap.

Fullerton stepped out into several feet of snow. Only then did he realize that the landing space didn't allow enough room for taking off in the heavily loaded Junkers. The aircraft had to be unloaded and flown to a small bay on the river where the ice was

smooth. As Fullerton flew towards the new landing, he heard an ominous knock in the engine. Either a valve, a ring or a piston was about to let go. Although he landed safely, it was decided to transfer *Vic*'s propeller and one of its skis to *Rene* and continue the flight to Fort Norman with one aircraft. The change-over was completed in a day, and the travellers said their goodbyes. No sooner had Gorman lifted off the snow than the engine stopped and the Junkers smashed into a snow-drift, breaking a wing and one ski and splintering the only surviving propeller. With no ability to communicate with the south, the expedition was stranded until the regular supply boats arrived in the summer. Disheartened, the flyers rented a cabin from Father Decoux, a Catholic missionary, and settled in for a long winter wait.

There were enough parts to put one aircraft back in the air, except for a propeller. The flyers were discussing the problem in the Hudson's Bay Company quarters one day when Philip Godsell, a Bay employee, suggested that they make another propeller. The idea seemed impractical until Godsell explained that all the necessary components were at hand, including oak sleigh boards and strips of moosehide that could be boiled down to make glue. There was a well-equipped workshop and an experienced cabinet-maker, Walter Johnson, who had a good set of hand tools. They decided to give it a try.

While the others repaired *Rene,* William Hill, the expedition's mechanic, collected the pieces of shattered propeller and began to work with Johnson to build a new prop. In the days that followed, templates were cut to shape, sleigh boards glued together and bound. Oak was shaped, sanded and balanced. Holes for the propeller boss were carefully drilled. Then the entire surface was sealed with an oil finish.

Opposite page; William Hill finishes the home-made propeller for Junkers F13 *Vic* at Fort Simpson, April 1921. (Public Archives of Canada, C 36391)

The new propeller was installed, and Fullerton started the motor. Slowly, he increased the throttle until the aircraft was straining against the tie-down ropes. There was no vibration. Hill and Johnson had done a perfect job. Fullerton shut down the engine and climbed out of the airplane. Expectant faces greeted him. "Well?" Fullerton smiled. "It's perfect!" The crew cheered, danced and hugged each other in the bitter cold. Hill and Johnson set to work promptly and produced a second propeller and two skis for the other Junkers.

The imminent breakup of ice on the Mackenzie River placed the two aircraft in considerable danger — they might be crushed by ice. A local trapper reported that the Liard River, a tributary of the mighty Mackenzie, had already broken. Fullerton warmed *Vic*'s engine and prepared for take-off. In the distance the pilots could hear the roar of breaking ice. Fullerton took off, narrowly missing the ice barrier, and flew the plane to a small lake. Gorman's take-off was less successful. *Rene*'s tail broke through the ice, and a team of oxen was brought in from the mission to pull the damaged aircraft out of the river.

Short of fuel, Fullerton flew back to Peace River in the serviceable Junkers with Gorman, Hill and Waddell. Derbyshire remained at Fort Simpson to work on the damaged *Rene.* Spring had already reached Peace River Crossing when Fullerton arrived. The snow was gone and the plane landed on the still ice-bound Little Bear Lake. There the Junkers was refitted with pontoons and a new propeller that had been brought up from the south. Once again they headed off to Fort Norman. This time the aircraft reached its destination, although one wing and a pontoon were damaged on landing. Despite numerous problems, the Junkers had proved their worth, and a first tentative step had been taken in commercial bush operations north of the sixtieth parallel, almost to the Arctic Circle.

By the end of the year *Rene,* badly damaged, had to be written off. *Vic* was stored in the small hangar at Peace River and advertised for sale. It was eventually bought by a group from Prince Rupert, British Columbia, to fly charter trips for prospectors and hunters into remote areas of the province. The venture failed, and the aircraft was resold and renamed *Prince George.* During a storm, while hauling gold from unofficial diggings in the province, the aircraft grounded on the rocky shore of Lake Stuart, and its pontoons were destroyed. Vandals eventually stripped what remained of the famous aircraft. The salvaged motor was converted into an air compressor for use at a local quartz mine. Then, it, too, vanished. The home-made propeller from *Rene* hung for many years over the fireplace in the Arizona home of George Gorman's widow. Hearing of its role in Canada's aviation history, Marion Gorman donated it to the National Aviation Museum in Ottawa, where it now resides.

At the end of 1921, all Alberta's private and fledgling commercial flying ventures were out of business. The leases on the May-Gorman airport lapsed. So did the leases on the Tailyour-McNeill airport facilities on Portage Avenue. Tall grass grew on both landing strips; the grass was cut for hay. Aircraft coming to Edmonton were rerouted to Fort Saskatchewan or Vegreville. With no aviation business to sustain his operations, Wop May handed the Jenny, *Edmonton*, back to the city. It sat ignominiously in a horse barn at the city's exhibition grounds. George Gorman gave up flying and left for California, where he opened a successful lumber business. May suffered a loss when his brother and business partner, Court May, tripped on the staircase of Edmonton's Macdonald Hotel, tumbled over the banister, and fell to

Wop May with Imperial Oil Junkers F13 *Vic* prior to change-over to pontoons, 1921. (City of Edmonton Archives, COE 10-2322)

his death on the marble floor below. In spite of the bad luck Wop carried on. He cared for little but aviation. He took a pilot refresher course at Camp Borden, then went to work as a mechanic for the Great Northern Flying Company. In slack periods he worked as a salesman.

In the east, meanwhile, Quebec aviation pioneer Joseph Pierre Romeo Vachon joined Laurentide as base air engineer at Lac la Tortue in 1922. The twenty-four-year-

Dayton-Wright FP-2 aircraft at Ottawa, Ontario, 1922. (Public Archives of Canada, PA 90271)

old Vachon had been an engineer afloat with the Royal Navy during the war. But Vachon's heart was in flying aircraft, not just maintaining them. Realizing the advantage of having a competent mechanic-pilot on staff, Laurentide sent him on a training course to the General Motors School of Aviation in Dayton, Ohio, where he obtained his commercial pilot's licence. Thereafter he flew one of the company's Curtiss HS-2L flying-boats. He became Quebec's earliest bush pilot and the country's first licensed pilot-engineer.

In 1924 things began picking up. Incorporated officially on April Fool's Day, the Royal Canadian Air Force emerged as the junior service of the armed forces. To equip it, eight Vickers Viking IV flying-boats were ordered. Along the west coast, these RCAF aircraft were used to patrol for illegal commercial fishing and apprehend rum-runners racing high-powered speedboats across the Strait of Juan de Fuca to the thirsty American markets around Puget Sound. From Victoria Beach Station (High River), Alberta, an RCAF Vickers Viking completed an aerial survey of the Churchill River districts and Reindeer Lake, covering

fifteen thousand square miles in less than a month. (Throughout the 1930s, the RCAF remained mainly a civil flying operation, performing such tasks as forestry patrols, photographic surveys and law enforcement. Most of its operations were conducted from the seaplane bases it inherited from the Air Board.)

The Province of Ontario created its own private air force and bush operation in 1924 with thirteen Curtiss HS-2L flying-boats, sixteen pilots and nineteen maintenance engineers. Based in Sault Ste. Marie, Ontario, the aircraft were used for fire patrol, personnel transportation, ambulance work and surveys. One pilot on forest fire

Curtiss HS-2L flying-boat of the Ontario Provincial Air Service. (Public Archives of Canada, PA 90266)

patrol on 5 July, 1924, flew for an incredible 10 hours 40 minutes. By the end of its first year, men and machines had spotted 597 fires, flown 170,000 air miles and logged 2,595 hours in the air.

There was a renewed interest in aviation that year in the west, as Wop May had anticipated. Harry Adair, a wealthy farmer in Grand Prairie, decided to invest in air transport. He was certain that, within a decade, it would overtake rail travel. He bought a new Curtiss Jenny in San Diego and hired May to fly it. The unused strip on Portage Avenue was cleared of weeds and grass and put back into service as home base for the Edmonton and Grand Prairie Aircraft Company. There was a brief setback when Adair, at the controls of the overloaded Jenny, and his passenger Harry Barr, a fur dealer, hit some telephone wires on take-off and crashed into a building. Both men escaped without injury, but May was forced to postpone a scheduled air tour until the Jenny was repaired. The accident demonstrated the need

for better airport facilities. Edmonton's new aviation-minded mayor, Ken Blatchford, with prompting from Adair and May, persuaded the city council to develop a long-term plan for a permanent and proper airport.

Not all pilots shared in the new aviation boom. After a stint in Ottawa working for the Soldier Settlement Board, Matt Berry tried farming near Rimbey, Alberta. The farm failed. Walter Gilbert managed to wrangle a flying refresher course at Camp Borden, then joined a mining survey business. Punch Dickins, who had won a DFC during the war, worked for General Motors for a time before rejoining the air force. Jack Bowen, who had been too young to fight in France, sailed with his brother down the Athabasca and Mackenzie rivers. They took a trip to Aklavik, on the Arctic Ocean,

Curtiss HS-26s at Sioux Lookout, Ontario, 1924. (Public Archives of Canada, C 62093)

44

which took three months, during which time the brothers learned how to live off the land. Later, Bowen became Wop May's navigator and engineer.

Bush flying was a game for young men. In 1924, none of the aviators had reached his thirtieth birthday. To survive and endure in the hostile environment of the north required a combination of great physical and mental strength, boundless optimism and a measure of good luck. There were no detailed maps, no long-distance airborne radios, no system of weather reporting, no general meteorological forecasting, and no help if a pilot went down. The farther north one flew, the more unreliable the compass became as its needle tilted towards the north magnetic pole. Above the sixty-fifth parallel of latitude, a compass could be wildly inaccurate. Navigation became a matter of dead reckoning — DR, it was called — based on a combination of factors: weather, winds aloft, visibility, fuel supply, cargo and courage. The wonder of it was that any of these early pioneers survived at all.

Twenty-year-old Jack Caldwell and his engineer were typical. Caldwell came from Lacombe, Alberta. He learned to fly in Calgary, then hauled prospectors into the remote mountainous regions of northern British Columbia and the Yukon in a Vickers Viking amphibian. Caldwell's engineer, Irene Vachon (no relation to Romeo Vachon in Quebec), had spent a season on aerial forestry patrols. The Viking aircraft had been sold to a group of Calgary businessmen interested in gold exploration. Calling themselves the Northern Syndicate Limited, the businessmen had been hooked by the gold bug through an old prospector whose single asset turned out to be a large jar of high-grade gold quartz he claimed to

Punch Dickins was the first pilot to reach the Arctic Circle. He brought back the first aerial shipment of furs from Fort Good Hope, 1924. (City of Edmonton Archives, A81-26)

Canadian Vickers Varuna
flying-boat of the RCAF at
Shirley's Bay, British
Columbia. (Public Archives
of Canada,   HC 843)

have dug up in the Barrenlands. He told an elaborate story.

His title to the claim was unregistered and required some surface staking work. His Indian wife had been left behind to guard the location, which the prospector had made clearly visible from the air by placing a cross of giant boulders on the site before he left. All he asked from the syndicate was a small advance, faith money, really. The businessmen dug into their collective pockets and ponied up the required sum. The old prospector announced solemnly that they were now partners. Everybody shook hands. The businessmen went back to their offices, and the prospector headed off to visit a few Calgary bars and celebrate his good fortune. During the last of several drunken brawls, someone hit him on the head with a bottle, and he lapsed into a coma, which lasted for several days. The anxious businessmen were at his hospital bedside when he regained consciousness. Unfortunately, the blow to his head had affected his memory, and he could no longer remember where his claim was. "Somewhere east of Great Slave Lake in the Barrenlands" was the best he could manage.

This unexplored region, known as Canada's blind spot, was an area three times the size of Europe, an inhospitable land of innumerable shallow lakes and rocky outcroppings, without mountains or trees, featureless, formless, forsaken. The syndicate members were determined to find the claim. The Vickers Viking, named the *Bouncing Bronco,* was shipped by rail northeast of Edmonton to Lac la Biche, where Caldwell and Vachon assembled and rigged the plane for their flight into the Barrens. Food supplies, aircraft parts, oil and fuel caches were arranged at various pick-up points along the proposed flight routes.

During the long daylight hours of July and August 1925, the young airmen crisscrossed the vast emptiness of the Barrens searching for a sign of a rocky cross and an adjoining Indian encampment. Once Caldwell thought he saw smoke and flew down to investigate. It turned out to be dust churned by a herd of wandering caribou. As freeze-up approached, Caldwell turned the aircraft south to High River. There the Viking was stored for the winter. In Calgary, the businessmen called it quits and sold the amphibian to a pilot in British Columbia.

The new owner used a low-grade oil and, after a few hours of flying, burned out the engine. The machine was abandoned behind a hangar at the Vancouver airport, where it slowly disintegrated. A gold prospector bought what was left and had it rebuilt. On a flight over the Fraser River a fuel line broke and the engine burst into flames. The alert pilot dived for the water, sideslipping to keep the flames from consuming the fuselage. A few feet above the river he flared out and made a rough but successful landing. People with small boats rescued everyone before the flaming Viking sank.

After the *Bouncing Bronco* was salvaged and sold, Jack Caldwell went by train and boat to Newfoundland, where he was hired to fly a ski-equipped Avro two-seater to spot seal herds for the commercial seal hunters on the off-shore ice fields. It was an experiment designed to prove to sceptical sealing captains the advantages of using an aircraft as a tool. The Avro was taken by a sealing ship to the general area of the hunt, then lowered over the side onto the ice. Caldwell took off, and within ten minutes found the main herd. The sealers got a record catch.

Seal spotting was dangerous and nerve-wracking work. There was no radio communication with the mother vessel. Thick fog could appear suddenly on the ice floes, and visibility would drop to zero. Disorientation sometimes occurred in white-out conditions when the sky and sea ice merged in an optical illusion and the horizon disappeared. An engine failure over water meant certain death within minutes. Caldwell arranged with the ship's captain to keep black smoke pouring from the funnel as a beacon whenever he was in the air. The six-week hunt ended without incident, and the sealers returned to St. John's delighted by Caldwell's contribution to their annual harvest.

Harold Oaks was a student at the University of Toronto when he first became aware of aviation's potential for mining exploration and development. A natural pilot with superb organizational skills, Oaks was unable to find a job that combined mining engineering with flying. He had decided to try his luck in South America when fate intervened. A wartime friend, Gerald Thompson, persuaded him to join the Ontario Provincial Air Service (OPAS). Because he was better educated than anyone else at the OPAS base in Sudbury, Oaks was derisively called Doc. The name stuck.

Early in 1926 he succumbed to the gold fever sweeping northern Ontario and took a leave of absence from OPAS. Oaks and Thompson travelled by dog team to join the rush to Red Lake. They staked several parcels of claims in the area, which they sold later for a handsome profit. Oaks used his share to purchase a minority interest in Patricia Airways and Exploration Company, based in Sioux Lookout, Ontario, on the CNR's main line. He set to work proving that an aviation business could be a sound economic enterprise. The less adventurous Thompson returned to OPAS.

Oaks arranged to purchase an open cockpit Curtiss Lark for his company, a machine capable of operating on skis or floats. Sam Thomlinson was hired on as maintenance engineer. During late summer of 1926 the plane flew up to ten trips a day into Red Lake, carrying prospectors and their supplies. Pat Airways, as it came to be known, with Doc at the helm, provided regular passenger, freight and mail service to Red Lake and Woman Lake throughout that year. Doc's airmail service charged twenty-five cents per letter and operated without government subsidy. By the time freeze-up arrived, Oaks had proved his point: a profitable air service could be operated successfully with good equipment, good service and sensible management. But Oaks wanted something better than a shoe string

H.S. (Doc) Oaks with his Curtiss Lark of Patricia Airways Exploration Ltd. at Red Lake, Ontario, 1926. (Public Archives of Canada, PA 89694)

bush operation. He resigned from the company.

Oaks met with John Wilson, Canada's Controller of Civil Aviation, in Ottawa and explained his ideas for a northern air service. Wilson suggested a meeting with Winnipeg industrialist and grain merchant James Richardson. The wealthy financier was an enthusiastic supporter of aviation. Richardson sounded like the sort of man Oaks had been looking for. He thanked Wilson and took the train to Winnipeg.

Richardson had just bankrolled Central Canada Airlines Limited in northern Ontario, operated by Jack Clarke, a pilot he had met while on vacation at Minaki Lodge. Clarke's Curtiss HS-2L flying-boat carried passengers and cargo about the region. However, when Richardson discovered that the flamboyant Clarke was more pilot than businessman, his enthusiasm for the venture cooled.

Above: WCA base at
Hudson, Ontario, 1927.
(Provincial Archives of
Manitoba, 1596)

Opposite page: James
Richardson, president of
Western Airways. He
gave his company wide
powers of operation in air
services, aircraft
manufacturing and
research. Later he
became known as the
Father of Canadian
Aviation, 1927.
(Provincial Archives of
Manitoba, 601)

Right: WCA office at
Gold Pines, Ontario,
1927. (Provincial
Archives of Manitoba,
406)

Above: Fokker Super Universal at Cold Lake, Manitoba, docked at Durie & Akers general store. (Provincial Archives of Manitoba, MA 601)

Below: First commercial flight of *City of Winnipeg*, 26 December, 1926. (Provincial Archives of Manitoba, 402)

Fred Stevenson loads the first editions of the *Winnipeg Evening Tribune* from newspaper executive Sam Sigesmund for delivery to mining camps in the Red Lake district. Later, when the affable Stevenson was killed in an air crash, the city of Winnipeg named its new airport after him. (Provincial Archives of Manitoba, 1665)

In Winnipeg, Oaks went straight from the railway station to the floor of the Winnipeg Grain Exchange and had Richardson paged. Each man recognized in the other a kindred spirit. Oaks had the credentials to prove he had that rare combination of business ability and flying skills necessary to organize and operate a successful national aviation company. Over dinner they formulated a working relationship for a new company, Western Canada Airways Limited (WCA). Base of operations for the company was to be at Hudson, on the south shore of Lost Lake. Oaks became manager and hired Al Cheeseman as base mechanic. For aircraft they chose a pair of new Fokker Universal monoplanes powered with recently developed radial air-cooled engines. The somewhat impractical Fokker had an open cockpit and employed a tail skid. It carried four passengers. The new acquisitions were ferried from New York to Hudson without incident.

Design development for the new radial air-cooled engine had been sponsored by the US Navy on the theory that a lighter, more reliable motor would translate into smaller and more efficient aircraft, which could be carried on naval vessels. Pratt & Whitney won the contract in 1926. Their radial air-cooled engines, with minor improvements, remained the power source for most aircraft until the introduction of turboprop and jet engines in the early 1950s. High-wing cabin monoplanes with fixed undercarriages powered by the new engines began to replace the slow, lumbering biplanes with their in-line engines. The high-wing monoplane design became the industry standard until 1932, when low-wing aircraft with retractable undercarriages were introduced.

There had been technical innovations in aircraft propellers as well. At Camp Borden in 1927, a successful air test of the first controllable-pitch propeller took place. Its inventor, W.R. Turnbull, a middle-aged engineer and tinkerer from Rothesay, New Brunswick, developed the idea in his home-built wind tunnel. His discovery finally made it possible for a pilot to use take-off power to climb to cruising altitude with his propeller in flat pitch, then reduce engine power and, from the cockpit, change the propeller's angle of attack to a coarser pitch for cruising. The controllable-pitch propeller improved the use of available engine power so planes required less space for take-off on land or water and gave pilots a faster control response. The new propeller also delivered a significant increase in aircraft range, since less fuel was required to cover the same distance than was needed with a fixed-pitch propeller. Best of all, there was less wear and tear on the engines. Most time in the air could be spent loafing along at low RPM with propellers in a coarse pitch.

Most of the courageous starry-eyed amateurs who had done so much during the

Fokker Tri-motor. (Canadian Aviation Museum, CAM 4992)

Oil derrick and drill flown in from Cache Lake to Fort Churchill by WCA. (Provincial Archives of Manitoba, 2241)

early years of aviation development had left the scene. The era of firsts by aviation pioneers was drawing to a close. One notable achievement in September 1926 was a trans-Canada seaplane flight by Canadian Squadron Leader Earl Godfrey and J. Dalzell McKee, a wealthy American. It was the first time an airplane had covered the distance from Montreal to Vancouver. In gratitude for the assistance given by the various air stations and bases *en route*, McKee established a silver trophy to commemorate the event. The trophy was to be awarded annually to whoever was judged to have contributed the most to Canadian aviation. The Trans Canada Trophy became generally known in later years as the McKee Trophy. Doc Oaks was its first winner, in 1927, "in recognition of his work in organizing air services to outlying districts." Significantly, the first three winners were bush pilots, proof of the importance of these northern flyers to Canadian aviation.

Doc Oaks' new Fokkers proved their value almost immediately: a New York businessman needed some financial papers signed by a prospector in the gold fields at Narrow River. He sent Oaks a telegram at Hudson. Oaks flew to Narrow River and snow-shoed to the prospector's cabin. The two men trekked to the airplane and flew to Sioux Lookout, where the prospector signed the papers at the local bank. What might have once taken three weeks had been done in half a day.

WCA's first big contract involved transporting machinery and supplies from Winnipeg to the port of Churchill on the Hudson Bay during the building of the Manitoba railway spur. To ensure that the two aircraft performed as advertised Oaks

Upon completion of the Churchill operation to bring explosives and drilling equipment by air to the northern Manitoba port, the men responsible for its success line up for a picture in front of their Fokker. (l to r) Rod Ross, Fokker test pilot Lieutenant Bernt Balchen, Al Cheeseman and Fred Stevenson, 1927. (Provincial Archives of Manitoba, 411)

arranged with the Fokker Company to send its test pilot, Bernt Balchen, to join the operation temporarily.

Balchen, a Norwegian by birth, arrived in Hudson with three company mechanics. They followed a narrow path through the swirling snow to a shack with a WCA board sign over the entrance. The small shack served as administration office and freight shed for operations into the gold fields. Balchen entered the building stamping the snow from his feet and introduced himself and his mechanics to the four men who were gathered around a pot-belly stove. Through a veil of smoke, Rod Ross, WCA's bearded superintendent, bid them welcome.

Thomas William Siers, aircraft engineer and designer of the oil-dilution system in aircraft piston engines for use in cold-weather operations, 1940. (Provincial Archives of Manitoba, 1657)

Ross wore beaded moccasins and buckskin. The visitors were invited to warm themselves and meet mechanics Tom Siers and Al Cheeseman. Lanky Fred Stevenson sat telescoped into a chair behind the stove, sucking on a curved briar pipe, his moccasined feet resting comfortably on a shelf. He gave them a casual wave. One of the company mechanics from New York began to fidget. Finally, he asked: "Which door to the men's room?"

Stevenson frowned, uncoiled his legs and got to his feet. He ripped a few pages from an Eaton's catalogue hanging on the wall and handed them to the mechanic. He pointed to the front door. "Pick yourself a spot, sonny boy. You got the whole damn north out there."

In 1928, WCA received a major contract to supply men and materials for the final leg of the rail line to Hudson Bay. Oaks established a temporary base for the Fokkers at Cache Lake, 180 miles southwest of Churchill. Railway-construction engineers needed to complete a series of geological tests before deciding whether the line should end at Port Nelson or Churchill. A heavy churn drill and half a ton of dynamite were required for the tests. No commercial flyers were prepared to tackle the job. Oaks promised that WCA would deliver the goods.

Flying the open-cockpit Fokkers into Churchill's appalling winter weather conditions was not for the faint-hearted. Cold, moist winds blew in from Hudson Bay and sliced through the warmest clothing. Needle-pointed snow-pellet blizzards, roaring winds and dense sea fog were all part of the normal winter weather. On one trip an oil line broke in Stevenson's Fokker, fifty miles out of Cache Lake. He landed on a small frozen lake and spent the night in his sleeping bag inside the aircraft, serenaded by howling wolves. In the watery morning sun Stevenson saw footprints in the snow and followed them to a trapper's cabin. He warmed himself by the stove, then made arrangements with the trapper to travel by dog team to Cache Lake.

Along the trail the dogs gave out and Stevenson was forced to continue on snowshoes by himself. Walking was difficult because his ankle, broken earlier in a crash at Fort Frances, had never healed properly. On the third day, he limped into the base, hungry, frost-bitten and exhausted. The first thing he saw was the Fokker he had left behind. Balchen and Cheeseman explained that when he had failed to arrive on schedule they flew out to search and found the abandoned Fokker without oil. They filled the oil tank, and Cheeseman, who had only a few hours of experience as a pilot, took off, followed by Balchen in the other aircraft. Neither man had noticed the broken

oil line. Within minutes Cheeseman's over-heated engine caught fire and he was forced to land. He set down quickly in a clearing, repaired the break and continued on to Cache Lake.

A week later an undercarriage support was broken on take-off from Cache Lake when the plane hit an ice hump. Stevenson and Cheeseman dragged the machine to the campsite, then borrowed a railway hand car and pumped their way, with the broken parts, to the railway repair shop at Pikwitonel, Manitoba.

The geological test holes drilled through the ice and muskeg proved to the

Edmonton airport hangar, 1928. (Provincial Archives of Alberta, 68.78/16)

Left: Gas tin, chamois and funnel. Roy Brown refuelling his Fokker Universal the hard way at Cranberry Portage, Manitoba, 1928. (Public Archives of Canada, PA 102336)

Below: Inauguration of international airmail between Canada and the United States at St. Hubert Airport, Quebec, 1 October, 1928. (Public Archives of Canada, C 53679)

Walter E. Gilbert was one of
the first pilots to join Western
Canada Airways in Winnipeg.
(Provincial Archives of
Manitoba, 1527)

engineers that the rail line could be built to Churchill, making it a seaport for the shipment of prairie grain. WCA's success with this venture, the first major project of its kind in the north, encouraged James Richardson and Doc Oaks to expand westward into Saskatchewan and Alberta. Stevenson continued flying for WCA during the summer, hauling mining equipment and supplies. Early in the new year, while working with Sherritt-Gordon Mines, on a flight test with a Fokker over The Pas, Manitoba, he allowed his airspeed to drop. The aircraft stalled and spun into one of the town's side streets.

Stevenson was killed. In memory of his aviation exploits Winnipeg named its main airport Stevenson Field.

Doc Oaks was not satisfied with the skis manufactured by Fokker for WCA. They cracked too easily on ice humps and in slushy weather conditions. The standard procedure for a pilot when finished flying at the end of the day was to cut several short log poles, then taxi his aircraft over them.

Silas A. Cheeseman (l) shaking hands with Doc Oaks; the first two operating personnel of WCA, 1928. (Provincial Archives of Manitoba, 1477)

(If a plane was left on the snow, the skis might freeze to the surface during the night.) In the morning, the skis were knocked loose from their support poles and the aircraft taxied off. Most of the time this system worked well. But sometimes the slender skis broke. Oaks approached Carmen and Warner Elliot, in Sioux Lookout, for help. The Elliots were wood craftsmen. In their small shop they built boats, sleighs, toboggans and skis. Oaks suggested a new ski designed for aircraft; thicker, wider, stronger and reinforced to withstand the brutal punishment of winter bush flying.

The brothers went to work. In due course the Elliots produced a new standard aircraft ski for bush operations. Made entirely by hand, the varnished white ash skis had reinforced bottoms covered with copper alloy and were bound together with 1,400 rivets. So successful was the design that American Admiral Richard Byrd used Elliot skis on his three Antarctic expeditions.

Doc Oaks and Al Cheeseman devised

Western Canada Airways dock and office at Yellowknife, Northwest Territories, 1928. (Provincial Archives of Manitoba, 821)

Left: Cabin cockpit of Western Canada Airways Boeing B1E flying-boat. (Public Archives of Canada, PA 89005)

Opposite page: Boeing B-1E flying-boat of Consolidated Mining and Smelting Co. with prospecting party at Vernon Lake, Vancouver Island, 25 October, 1929. (Public Archives of Canada, PA 88791)

Below: Freighting by dog team from aircraft to Gold Pines, Ontario. Taken by Doc Oaks. (Provincial Archives of Manitoba, 434)

another improvement for bush operations: an all-weather canvas-covered nose hangar for servicing aircraft engines outdoors. They were immediately canonized by every pilot, mechanic, apprentice and dock-walloper who had ever frozen his fingers or fought off blackflies while working on an aircraft. Equipped with a stove, the small wooden-framed tent cabin was constructed on skids and enclosed on three sides with a canvas flap that folded neatly around the front of

the aircraft. In 1928, after WCA moved thirty tons of mining equipment and supplies to open up Sherritt-Gordon mining properties in Saskatchewan, Doc Oaks resigned from the company to form a partnership with Jack Hammell, a mining promoter. They formed Northern Aerial Minerals Exploration to develop prospective mining areas in the far north. In the first summer the company pilots flew one hundred thousand miles, to sites from Ungava Bay to the Yukon. In the

process they opened the Arctic so that lesser mortals could explore at their leisure. The company established thirty-three fuel caches to fly prospectors into the most remote and unexplored regions of the Canadian north.

When Oaks left WCA, James Richardson hired Leigh Brintnell away from the Ontario Provincial Air Service to fill the vacancy. Brintnell, a RFC veteran, had that rare combination of management and flying abilities needed by Richardson. Under Brintnell, WCA continued to expand. The company received a mail contract from the post office to provide service to remote areas of northwestern Ontario and Manitoba previously serviced by dog team. Brintnell carried out

the first WCA survey flight into Alberta late in 1928. He hired new pilots and bought new aircraft and expanded the company's operations west to the Rockies and east into Quebec.

A month after Stevenson's death, Great Western Airways (GWA), in Calgary, managed by the indomitable Fred McCall, received a contract to carry a hazardous cargo of nitroglycerine from Shelby, Montana, to Calgary. The highly explosive cargo was needed urgently to extinguish a fire burning out of control in the newly discovered Turner Valley oil fields. McCall figured he could move everything up to Calgary in four trips. On his first return flight from Shelby with nitroglycerine and twelve sticks of dynamite on board, the aircraft was buffeted by strong head winds. He approached the Calgary Aero Club's airfield with his fuel gauge needle on empty. No sooner had he landed than the motor burped once and died. If it had happened two minutes earlier McCall might have crashed in a gigantic explosion. Someone brought a gallon of gas so he could taxi to the hangar. The remaining three trips were made without incident and in calm weather. The Turner Valley oil fire was extinguished.

Opposite page: Leigh Brintnell peers from the cockpit of his Bellanca. Brintnell was a man of extraordinary drive and energy. His company, Commercial Airways, opened flying routes from Edmonton and Fort McMurray to the newly discovered mining areas around Great Bear Lake. (Public Archives of Canada, PA 102782)

Below: Captain Con Farrell dropped in to Fargo, North Dakota for fuel during the delivery flight of this new Fokker mail plane, 1929. (Provincial Archives of Manitoba, 699)

New Frontiers

Punch Dickins was one of the new pilots who joined Western Canada Airways. The twenty-nine-year-old Dickins' exploits were already a legend among bush pilots. Dominion Explorers Limited (Domex) hired Dickins for a four-thousand-mile flight into the north country. Dickins, engineer William Nadin, Charles MacAlpine, president of Domex, and Richard Pearce, the editor of the *Northern Miner*, left on a reconnaissance flight from Winnipeg in late August. Their new Fokker Super Universal seaplane G-CASK was the latest in aviation technology. Their first stop, Norway House, at the northern end of Lake Winnipeg, took four hours to reach. Beyond Norway House, Dickins ran

Official opening of Edmonton Municipal Airport, March 1927. (l) Punch Dickins and (r) Mayor Bury. (Public Archives of Canada, C 57671)

into heavy fog and was forced to put down on the Nelson River. When the fog lifted, he took off for Churchill, following the muddy Nelson and Churchill rivers. Beyond Churchill they crossed the tree line, hugging the bleak, rocky coastline. Below them they could see whales surfacing and sounding in the light green waters of Hudson Bay.

At Chesterfield Inlet, Dickins swung inland, following a chain of lakes. Chesterfield Inlet was thought to be a long, narrow bay. The flight showed it to be a 280-mile-long waterway, wide enough for ocean vessels. Dickins expected his to be the first aircraft to reach Chesterfield Inlet. He was startled to learn that bush pilot Duke Schiller had arrived the day before. The coincidental arrival of two aircraft within a

Punch Dickins's famous Fokker G-CASK lies on a tranquil forest-fringe lake. The aircraft carried the young pilot on his historic flight when he was the first to travel across the Barrens, 1928. (Public Archives of Canada, C 57532)

day of each other at the same location 1200 miles north of civilization was a clear indication of how quickly the north was opening to commercial interests.

On the next leg of their flight, Dickins crossed the Barrenlands to Lake Athabasca. Pearce described the bleak, unexplored, uninhabited landscape below: "Hour after hour as the Fokker droned westward we saw only lakes and rocks devoid of vegetation. For nearly three hundred miles the only living thing sighted was a seagull." Their navigational problems were formidable. Dickins planned to follow the landmarks provided by the region's main water courses. The only map available of the area had large blank spaces captioned in boldface type with the word "UNEXPLORED".

Dickins related that for the first hour he was able to pick out the large water courses of the Thelon River and Lake Whenton. After that, "there were fewer features or lakes, and the streams became smaller and practically disappeared, until I saw a large area of water, Lake Dubaunt. I knew we were crossing the height of land where the waters would start flowing south to Athabasca. The map of this route down to Lake Dubaunt was fairly accurate but from there on practically useless." For most of the way Dickins used the sun to navigate. One hundred miles out from Lake Athabasca, visibility dropped to less than a quarter of a mile in haze from western forest fires. Dickins landed on a lake fifty miles from Athabasca and waited until the visibility improved.

Next day the party flew on to Stony Rapids on the Cat River, where the local RCMP contingent, delighted for the company, put them up for the night. On the next leg, Stony Rapids to Fitzgerald, they ran into strong head winds and ran out of gas. They landed on the Slave River and built a raft to float the Fokker downstream. While the raft was under construction, the steamer *Northland Echo* appeared on the river and paused long enough to provide them with aviation fuel. The Fokker continued to its destination without further incident. The twelve-day round trip from Winnipeg resulted in large areas of the northern route being explored and recorded for pilots who came later to photograph the area and make the maps upon which every bush pilot would depend.

First airmail to leave Winnipeg for Regina and Calgary. Piloted by W.J. Buchanan, 1928. Note the hand-cranked camera filming the event. (Provincial Archives of Manitoba, 510)

Above: Avro Avian lll trainer at Kirkfield Park, Winnipeg. (Provincial Archives of Manitoba,2)

Below: Peace River, Alberta. Avro Avian of Commercial Airways used on the mercy flight to Fort Vermilion, January 1929. (Provincial Archives of Alberta, 18)

On New Year's Day, 1929, in Calgary, Wop May and his wife, Violet, were spending a quiet morning when the telephone rang. It was the province's Deputy Minister of Health, Dr. Malcolm Bow. He had received a desperate message for help from Dr. Harold Hamman in the community of Little Red River, six hundred miles north of Edmonton, at the junction of the Peace and Mikkwa rivers. Diphtheria had broken out among the residents. Hamman was out of vaccine and feared for the settlement's survival.

Only an aircraft could get the vaccine to him in time to save lives. Bow asked if May would help. May promised, "I'll take the next train to Edmonton."

Since there was no direct telegraph link between Edmonton and Little Red River, more than a week had elapsed since

Deputy Minister of Health, Dr. Bow, handing serum wrapped in a blanket to Wop May for his mercy flight to Fort Vermilion, 1929. (City of Edmonton Archives, A81-26)

Dr. Hamman's message went out. A local resident, Bill Grey, had carried it overland by horse and sleigh to Fort Vermilion, fifty-five miles southwest of Little Red River. There, Joe Lefleur and Bill Lambert, Lefleur's son-in-law, carried it more than two hundred miles south to the telegraph office at Peace River.

There were few aircraft in Edmonton capable of making such a trip in mid-winter. Western Canada Airways had withdrawn its Fokkers to Winnipeg until spring, and the RCAF Station at High River had closed down temporarily during the cold snap. Fortunately, the Edmonton and Northern Alberta Aero Club operated two types of trainers suitable for cold-weather operations: deHavilland Moths and an Avro Avian. May planned the flight details at the Aero Club with Cy Becker, the club's president, and pilot Vic Horner. May decided to use the open-cockpit Avian biplane. The little fabric-covered aircraft had an empty weight of less than eight hundred pounds and a top speed of one hundred miles per hour. To help out in case of trouble, Horner agreed to accompany May on the trip. Two days later they were ready.

May and Horner stood shivering at dawn on the morning of their departure. Each wore several layers of woollen long-johns and sweaters under a thick leather coat. Dr. Bow handed a small bundle wrapped in a tartan blanket to May. It contained six hundred thousand units of anti-toxin. It was stowed in the Avian's baggage compartment, where a charcoal-fired warmer had been installed by Ralph Brinkman, the Aero Club's mechanic, to prevent it from freezing. May climbed into the rear cockpit, Horner up front. Both pilots wore thick leather helmets, goggles, and silk and wool scarves wrapped around their faces to protect them from the frightful cold. Brinkman swung the propeller. The Cirrus engine settled into a comfortable bark. May waved away the chocks. A touch of throttle and G-CAVB taxied away to the take-off point. The deputy minister held his hat as he stood in the freezing slipstream. The ground temperature was -36°C. Dr. Bow could only imagine what the temperature would be aloft at one hundred miles per hour. A small crowd watched the departure. Some were

Avro Avian III at Brandon Avenue dock, Winnipeg, 1929. (Provincial Archives of Manitoba, 7)

Wop May and Vic Horner ready to leave on their mercy flight to Fort Vermilion, 1929. (City of Edmonton Archives, A81-26)

sure they would never see the aircraft or its occupants again. The *Edmonton Journal* called the trip foolhardy and accused the government of blatant disregard for the pilots' lives.

Once he had lifted the Avian into the air, May swung north, following the railway line to Peace River. Cloud layers kept them close to the ground most of the way.

Employees at various Hudson's Bay posts along the route had been notified by radio to provide help in case of an emergency. A new local radio station, CJCA, broadcast special bulletins to its listeners on the flight path May and Horner would be following.

Near noon May landed in a clearing to refuel from the extra tank they carried on board. The pilots paused for a few moments to stamp the circulation back into their cramped legs, eat some chocolate bars and sandwiches, and drink from a thermos of coffee before taking off again. After a few minutes in the air May sensed something was wrong and landed in the first open area. Smoke poured from the baggage compartment. The flyers leaped out, ripped open the compartment hatch and quickly stifled the smouldering blankets with handfuls of snow. Loose coals from the charcoal warmer had ignited the blanket protecting the vaccine. Without heat the vaccine would freeze. The pilots decided to use their body heat to protect the vials, carefully stuffing them under their arms, into pockets and close to their groins. They reached McLennan, a small railroad community, in the last light of that short winter day. A runway had been marked out with spruce boughs on a lake close to the town.

Residents helped the men out of the aircraft. The engine oil was drained and

stored, with the vials of vaccine, at the McLellan Hotel, where May and Horner warmed themselves with hot soup. Next day at first light they returned to the Avian where Horner warmed the oil over an open fire while May waved a blow torch over the frozen engine. When some of their precious oil spilled accidentally, they quickly shovelled the congealed snow into cans and boiled the contents until all the water vapour was gone, then poured the oil into the engine.

In the biting cold they flew on to Peace River where they refuelled. By this time both men were physically exhausted and suffering from leg cramps. May sent a message to CJCA radio, asking the station to advise its listeners at Fort Vermilion that they would be arriving that afternoon. He suggested that a dog team be sent out to meet the aircraft at Peace River if the storm that was brewing made flying impossible and forced them to turn back. The local police force sent a second message to CJCA, asking them to instruct the constable at Fort Vermilion to head out along the aircraft's intended route by dog team if the Avian failed to make the settlement by nightfall.

The hastily prepared runway at Peace River had filled with snow already, and although sleighs had been used to pack down its surface, it took much longer to take off than May had anticipated. The Avian staggered into the air. May saw the railway bridge that spanned the river directly ahead. There was no time to climb above it. Instead, he pushed down the nose and flew between the bridge supports, holding the aircraft at between fifty and a hundred feet above the frozen river to maintain visibility. Through the blizzard and gale-force winds the pilots buffeted their way between the river banks, trying to hold a centre course. Then the motor coughed and died. The Avian slanted for the frozen river. Moments before touchdown, and quite inexplicably, the engine suddenly backfired and resumed normal operation. May eased the Avian to altitude and pressed on through the storm. They flew all day.

As daylight faded Horner caught sight of a marked landing strip beside a snow-covered building at Fort Vermilion. They circled and landed. It took several RCMP officers to lift the pilots out of their frozen cockpits and help them into a waiting sled. They were taken to the Mountie barracks to thaw out and were given hot food. Within

Dog teams at Fort Vermilion, 1929. (City of Edmonton Archives, A81-26)

MODER
STUD
EDMONTON

the hour Dr. Hamman arrived from Little Red River to announce that the crisis was over. Only one man had died, Albert Logan, a Hudson's Bay Company employee. The trip had been for nothing.

Hamman was sorry to have put the flyers through such an ordeal. "I felt a great relief when I saw them arrive safely, but I also felt very badly. I was responsible for these men endangering their lives."

Return from mercy flight. (l to r) Babe Horner, Vic Horner, Violet May and Wop May. (City of Edmonton Archives, A81-26)

Their flight home was unpleasant. A poor grade of fuel was taken on at Fort Vermilion. Once airborne, the Cirrus engine kept stopping and starting. May and Horner realized that an emergency landing without supplies in the northern wilderness during

January was as good as a death warrant. By the time they reached Peace River, the Avian's instruments were frozen and the fuel tank held less than a gallon. The exhausted pair refuelled, paused for some food, then flew on.

Edmonton had been told of their departure and estimated time of arrival by radio from Fort Vermilion. Crowds began to gather at the airport. At the Aero Club, Cy Becker decided to fly out to meet May and Horner in one of the club's Moths. Bad weather forced him to turn back. As he taxied in from the aborted flight, spectators thought he was May and descended on the aircraft. Hundreds of cars gathered around Blatchford Field, where police had set up barricades to control the crowd.

Finally, May and Horner arrived. They stared in amazement at the spectacle below. The Avian turned on its final approach. Neither man realized that their names had become known from coast to coast. Overnight, they had become national heroes. May slid onto the runway in a perfect landing and started to taxi towards the hangar. A great mob of well-wishers began running to the aircraft. Quickly, May swung the Avian around and taxied to the end of the runway, where he shut off the engine. The crowd engulfed the aircraft. Strong hands lifted the pilots out of their cockpits and onto waiting shoulders; they were carried in triumph to the hangar. When May removed his leather helmet, the silk scarf had frozen to his face. As he pulled it away skin peeled from his nose and lips. Babe Horner and Violet May joined their husbands and were immediately swamped by newspapermen and photographers asking them to pose beside the Avian. Well-wishers pumped the pilots' numb hands and shouted with enthusiasm. Police estimated later that ten thousand people had turned out to greet the flyers. May and Horner were stunned.

Later, on the train home to Calgary, May observed to his wife: "If the mercy flight achieved nothing else it proved once and for all that aircraft are a vital lifeline to remote communities that are cut off for days and weeks at a time from their neighbours to the south."

Search and Rescue

Colonel C. MacAlpine, president of the Dominion Explorers Club in Winnipeg, was an aggressive visionary who realized the enormous potential of using aircraft to prospect the gigantic unmapped and unexplored areas of the far north. In the summer of 1929 MacAlpine organized the most ambitious private aerial exploration operation in the western hemisphere. He intended to fly into the far north with two aircraft and cover twenty thousand miles of unknown territory. Seven men in two planes, a Fairchild, operated by the Explorers Club, and a Fokker Super Universal, leased from Western Canada Airways, took off in front of

Vickers Vista seaplane. (Public Archives of Canada, HC 1661)

the commercial wharf on the Red River near Winnipeg, and banked towards the north. Twenty-five-year-old RCAF-trained Stan McMillan flew the club's Fairchild, while Tommy Thompson piloted the Fokker.

Colonel MacAlpine, engineer Don Goodwin, and Richard Pearce, editor of the *Northern Miner*, who had crossed the Barrens with Punch Dickins, flew with Thompson. Aircraft engineer Alex Milne and Ed Boadway, a mining engineer and pilot, flew with McMillan. MacAlpine's plan called for the explorers to fly to Churchill on Hudson Bay, then on to Baker Lake, finally skirting the

Gas barrel, wobble pump, hose, chamois and funnel. Refuelling a Fairchild of Northern Aerial Mineral Exploration Ltd. the easy way, 1928. (Public Archives of Canada, C 62052)

Arctic coast to Aklavik where the mighty Mackenzie River emptied into the Arctic Ocean. From Aklavik they planned to make short hops into the Yukon, picking up prospectors. They would then start back for Winnipeg past Great Slave Lake, past Great Bear Lake, past The Pas, Manitoba. It all sounded good on paper. However, shortly after they took off from Winnipeg things began to go wrong.

Dense smoke from forest fires burning out of control stung their eyes and cut visibility to less than a mile. The pilots flew lower to try to maintain visual contact with the ground, until finally they were skimming the tree tops in visibility of less than a couple of hundred yards. They landed several times to check their bearings, but had only the vaguest idea of where they were. They continued north, flying blind in the smoke and using the compass to hold direction. Eventually, low on fuel, they crossed Lake Winnipeg and put down at Jackfish Island for fuel. But someone had been there before them. The cache was empty. They pushed on towards Churchill in the haze, their eyes shifting anxiously between the gas gauges, the ground and the clock. Finally, a few miles short of Churchill, the haze began to clear and they broke out into bright sunshine. They landed with only a few drops of fuel left. The Fokker was anchored offshore for the night; the Fairchild was tied to an RCAF buoy. In Churchill they were told that the *Morso*, a supply schooner chartered by the Explorers Club, had not arrived. The colonel decided to send the two aircraft out to look for it next day.

Early the following morning dredging crews reported that only the Fairchild remained in the harbour. During the night the Fokker had apparently been taken out to sea on a strong ebb tide. The *Acadia*, an oceanographic vessel taking soundings at the harbour entrance, sighted the half-submerged Fokker and steamed to the rescue. Unfortunately, when crewmen attempted to lift the machine onto the ship, the cables slipped and the aircraft broke up and promptly sank. Later, when the *Acadia* raised its anchor, the crew discovered the wrecked Fokker hooked to its anchor chain.

The mystery of the missing supply schooner was solved near dusk, when Eskimos sighted two of the *Morso*'s boats making for the harbour. The survivors explained that they had abandoned the ship when it caught fire. As the vessel carried a considerable cargo of dynamite among its supplies, the crew judiciously took to the boats before the ship blew up. Next day strong tides dragged the Fairchild and its anchor buoy out to sea, where it was recovered by a tug. To prevent similar accidents, McMillan flew the Fairchild to Baker Lake. Milne, Boadway and the others awaited a replacement for the wrecked Fokker. Eight days later, pilots Roy Brown and Robert Baker arrived in Churchill with G-CASK, a second WCA Fokker Super Universal.

Frustrated by the delays, MacAlpine ordered Thompson to fly to Baker Lake. From there the pilots prepared for the long flight to Bathurst Inlet on the Arctic Ocean. Carburetor troubles grounded the aircraft for half a day, but both machines managed to make Beverly Lake before dark. The men unpacked their sleeping bags and bedded down on the tundra under the stars for the night. In the morning they set course due north for Bathurst Inlet. For four hours, bucking head winds and snow squalls, they droned above the myriads of lakes and flat featureless landscape. The weather continued to deteriorate, until they had only the occasional glimpse of the sun by which to navigate. The pilots crept lower, sliding between cloud layers for glimpses of the ground. Head winds increased, until their ground speed slowed to a crawl. They decided to land on the nearest navigable lake and wait until the storm blew itself out.

No sooner were they down than the temperature began to plummet and a layer of thin ice began to form along the shore line. What to do? If they remained overnight there was a danger of the aircraft being frozen in for the winter; if they continued on in head winds they could run out of fuel before they reached Bathurst Inlet. Carefully, they checked the aircraft fuel tanks with a dipstick. They decided that they had three hours of fuel left in the tanks. When the wind dropped they took off immediately and climbed through the clouds into smoother air. The cloud cover grew thicker then parted momentarily, providing a quick peek of what lay below. They were over a large lake filled with pieces of drifting ice, and assumed that they had reached the coastline near Bathurst Inlet. In reality, they were well northeast of Bathurst Inlet at Dease Point, near the mouth of the Koolgaryuk River.

They followed the coast until they passed over an Eskimo settlement, a collection of flat-topped earth mounds near the shore. Everyone decided it was time to stop and regroup. The aircraft landed in front of the encampment and taxied to the beach, where a group of curious Eskimos had gathered. Grateful for human companionship and knowing the Eskimos would help them, the flyers pitched their tents for the night and wriggled into their sleeping bags.

Next morning, through sign language,

they learned from their hosts that the nearest Hudson's Bay Company store lay at Cambridge Bay, four hours away by boat. Joe, a young Eskimo, agreed to guide them to the post. With a nervous Joe strapped in the front seat beside him, McMillan took off in the Fairchild to find the post. Once airborne Joe relaxed and easily identified the route. But fog set in before they reached their destination and McMillan was forced to turn back to save fuel. It was to be their last chance of getting out by air. The Eskimos waved aside any suggestion of starting out on foot or by boat until after freeze-up. They would have to wait until they could cross the strait and reach the Hudson's Bay

MacAlpine party marooned at Dease Point. (l to r) Ed Boadway, Stan McMillan, Don Goodwin, Alex Milne, Col. C.H.D. MacAlpine, an Eskimo guide named Joe, George Thompson and Major R. F. Baker, 1929. (Provincial Archives of Manitoba, 2147)

post on foot.

Colonel MacAlpine, as always, rose to the occasion. Assignments to ensure their survival were handed out to each member of the expedition. The men settled down to a lengthy wait, passing the time learning what they could of the Eskimo language and the customs of the people. They built a sod hut with a tent at one end to protect them from the mind-numbing winds that swept down unceasingly from the high Arctic. After a few days the structure collapsed during a violent snowstorm. The Eskimos helped them rebuild it. A makeshift stove was attempted, using an engine cowling, much to the amusement of the Eskimos. The flyers' main problem was how to cook their food. Their stomachs were not accustomed to the local diet of raw fish and blubber. Fortunately, the enterprising McMillan managed to trade a pair of binoculars for an Eskimo tin stove. Moss and willow twigs were used as fuel. It smoked like hell, but it worked. As the food supply dwindled, the men were forced to supplement their diet with rancid dried salmon and whitefish generously provided by the Eskimos. Although the fish produced violent stomach cramps it kept them from starving. Occasionally, one of them managed to bring down a ptarmigan and treated everyone to a few morsels of fresh meat.

One day they awoke to find that the Eskimos had decamped. They were alone. They realized how much they had come to depend upon these unique people for survival and companionship. Years later Stan McMillan remembered vividly his sense of utter isolation that morning when he found the Eskimos had gone without explanation. A few days later they returned as mysteriously as they had disappeared. They offered no explanations but introduced a newcomer in their midst who spoke a little English and called himself Charlie. With a wide smile Charlie informed them that they had landed on Queen Maud Gulf and that, when the ice was strong enough, they could cross to Cambridge Bay and make contact with the white man's civilization. The weeks crawled by.

Even with the supplemental food provided by the Eskimos, their stores continued to shrink at an alarming rate. The flyers began to lose weight, and they became lethargic as the spectre of starvation appeared. Baker developed an agonizing tooth abscess which Pearce lanced with a penknife sterilized in rum. Mild weather returned early in October; the snow melted, which dampened their spirits. Once again the Eskimos vanished into the bleak landscape. They returned eleven days later. Eskimo Charlie explained their absence as a hunting expedition, and gave the white men part of their catch. Pearce, who had agreed earlier to trade his pocket watch for a fresh caribou, decided instead to trade the timepiece for some stale meat. By mid-October temperatures again dropped, and the flyers were enormously cheered at the prospect of an imminent departure. They spent the last night with their Eskimo guides in the crowded shack that had been their home for so many weeks.

Next morning, with guides, sleds and dog teams, they set out for Cambridge Bay, confident of reaching the Hudson's Bay post by nightfall. But the long weeks of inactivity and irregular diet had taken their toll. An hour after starting across the ice they were close to exhaustion. By nightfall they had barely enough strength left to help the Eskimos build an igloo to shield them from the wind. Near midnight the igloo collapsed, and they were forced out of their sleeping bags to rebuild it. Next day the trek continued. They staggered forward over ice rifts, snow drifts and hummocks. After three days of frustration and backbreaking work they were still on the peninsula, and nearly out of supplies. They shared the frozen fish intended for the sleigh dogs. Their guides decided to turn back to Dease Point for more food. The flyers waited patiently for their return.

The last week of October turned bitterly cold. The men celebrated Hallowe'en with some dried fish and a teaspoon of cocoa powder mixed in a pot of hot water. Eskimo Charlie and the other guides appeared the next day, bringing tobacco, flour and a report that someone had heard an aircraft flying over the Dease Point encampment. The men, thinking of their families, debated whether this was good news or bad.

The nightmare journey across the ice continued. Patches of thin ice lay along the route. The Eskimos used spears to test the thickness. Alice, wife of one of the Eskimo guides, broke through up to her knees. The flyers watched in amazement as she pitched forward into the freezing water and lay motionless, arms spread, to keep from sinking. McMillan described the event later. "She lay flat until one of the Eskimos pulled her out. We went on for a little while and then Alice changed out of her wet clothes in the open."

As they pushed forward, Alice's three-year-old son kept falling from the sled. She removed the boy's clothes and tied him to her bare back under her parka. The woman appeared indifferent to the extra weight and continued walking at the same pace as the others. The flyers developed great respect and an extraordinary sense of humility in the presence of their benefactors. Five miles short of their destination, thin ice again barred their way. Eskimo Charlie explained that they had two choices: turn back or make a dash for it. The flyers opted for the dash. Charlie cautioned them that, once they started on the run, they could not stop or they would drop through into the freezing water. Nor could any of them pause to help a casualty. The group of sleighs, dogs, men and women started the dash.

Pearce wrote: "The dogs were urged by word and lash to keep moving. My second wind passed without recognition and I was running on my fifth about the second mile or so. How we kept moving I don't know. We simply had to." They staggered onto the safe ice and dropped from exhaustion. A salty slush on the ice surface penetrated their moccasins and froze their socks. All were suffering from frostbitten faces, toes, fingers and wrists. The dogs collapsed from exhaustion. In the distance they could make out the mast of the *Bay Maud*, a Hudson's Bay Company ship purchased from the Norwegian explorer Roald Amundsen. The men drew from their last reservoir of strength and lurched forward to salvation.

Crewmen helped them aboard the vessel. Eskimo Charlie and his friends were paid off with a handsome credit for goods at the Hudson's Bay Company store, along with profuse thanks. All members of the expedition were suffering from the effects of scurvy: the fillings had fallen out of their teeth and their faces, hands and feet had swelled. On board the *Bay Maud*, the famished Pearce, Baker and MacAlpine began to eat. MacAlpine started by downing three cans of tomatoes. Next, he and the others each packed away six eggs, bacon and three quarters of a raisin pie. Later that night they climbed out of their bunks and went back to the galley for a snack, stuffing themselves with chocolates. By morning they were all sick. A diet of tinned tomatoes and grapefruit brought them back to health.

Meanwhile, the outside world's attention was focused on Wall Street, where the ten-year bull market had finally crashed, setting the stage for the global depression that was to follow. Initially, the missing men were given scant attention by the media. The last radio message received from MacAlpine's explorers had been from Baker Lake, when Tommy Thompson had advised that they were leaving for Bathurst Inlet in the morning. Later, the Hudson's Bay Company post at Bathurst Inlet radioed that the aircraft had not arrived. As the days turned into weeks with no news about the fate of the expedition, the newspapers picked up the story. Sensational headlines appeared in all the national newspapers, and for a time readers were spared reading about the calamities of Wall Street and treated instead to the disappearance of the MacAlpine expedition. Worried relatives and business associates of the expedition's members pushed for a search.

General David Hogarth, a long-time friend of MacAlpine, took it upon himself to organize one of the most elaborate aerial searches ever undertaken in the western hemisphere. From his temporary headquarters in the Winnipeg Grain Exchange, Hogarth persuaded Western Canada Airways and the Dominion Explorers group to pool their resources. Guy Blanchet, head of the Dominion Explorers operation, was put in charge of the search and sent to Stony Rapids with pilots Roy Brown and Albert Hollick-Kenyon, flying two WCA Fokkers. Dominion Explorers provided two Fairchilds, flown by Bill Spence and Charles Sutton. A third

group, Jimmy Vance, Pat Reid and Andy Cruickshank, kept the searchers supplied with fuel and supplies while the others looked for the missing men.

Working on the assumption that the expedition might be frozen in at one of the northern lakes, Brown and Spence flew to Baker Lake then to Pelly Lake and finally to Beverly Lake, where they found the supply cache that had been used by MacAlpine's expedition. Another possibility presented itself to the searchers. Perhaps the expedition had flown towards the coast and been forced to land after running out of fuel. The searchers decided to move the supply aircraft up to Baker Lake. Leigh Brintnell took

Opposite page: Bush pilot Albert Hollick-Kenyon. (Provincial Archives of Manitoba, 1555)

Below: Concentration of aircraft at Cranberry Portage, Manitoba, for the MacAlpine expedition search, 1929. (Provincial Archives of Manitoba, 437)

over co-ordination of WCA's activities from Winnipeg and the fleet of five float-equipped aircraft began looking from dawn to dark until the lakes froze. The searchers found no more clues to the lost expedition.

In three courageous trips into the far north from Edmonton during late September and early October, Punch Dickins added his considerable experience and abilities to the search. On his first trip with engineer Bill Tall he searched from Great Bear Lake to Coppermine River and to Coronation Gulf on the Arctic Ocean. On the return trip, Dickins picked up some stranded prospectors who had been waiting for the MacAlpine expedition and had all but given up hope of rescue. On his second trip he flew from Fort Fitzgerald to Bathurst Inlet and searched that area in a giant circle north of Great Slave Lake to the headwaters of the Coppermine River.

Dickins was flying a lone single-engine aircraft without proper maps, without an effective compass or blind-flying instruments, far from any supply depot, radio contact or human civilization, and in the worst weather imaginable, over some of the most desolate and rugged terrain on earth. He did this not once but three times in the space of two months. That he survived is remarkable; that he lived a full life and eventually died in his bed is nothing short of miraculous.

During October the aircraft at Baker Lake were grounded until the lakes froze and the ice thickened. Pontoons were taken off and skis put on. One night a few days before freeze-up a howling Arctic gale descended on Baker Lake, turning the surface into a tumultuous mass of freezing spray. Although the flyers managed to pull their aircraft up on shore, the tail assembly of Jimmy Vance's Fokker was damaged beyond repair. When the wind died, the search aircraft flew on to Burnside River to set up a new advance base and fuel cache.

Bill Spence touched down first, felt the rubbery ice under his skis and held his power until he reached the thicker ice inshore. Andy Cruickshank's landing was much more exciting. His aircraft broke through and sank. Fortunately, those on

Right: Pick-up of the MacAlpine expedition by two Fokker Super Universals at Cambridge Bay, Victoria Island, 6 November, 1929. Hudson's Bay vessel *Bay Maud* is in the background. (Provincial Archives of Manitoba, 550)

Opposite page: J. Roy Brown, member of the MacAlpine search team, 1929. (Provincial Archives of Manitoba, 1455)

board were able to scramble to safety through the hatch above the pilot's seat. Later, Cruickshank returned to Burnside, salvaged the machine and flew it back to Winnipeg.

By late October the ski-equipped aircraft were in the air. The operation was plagued by continuous bad weather and aircraft maintenance problems. Low ceilings kept Spence and Brown from leaving Bathurst Inlet to search the area along the north coast of the Kent Peninsula as far as Cambridge Bay. Finally, the weather lifted. Just as the aircraft were ready to depart a dog team appeared in the distance. An Eskimo brought a written radio message for transmission to Winnipeg. The MacAlpine expedition members had been found and were safe. The three search aircraft left Bathurst Inlet to pick them up.

Along the way they ran into heavy mist and fog and were forced to land on the ice between an island and the shore to wait for visibility to improve. When the weather cleared they took off. However, Spence forgot to switch fuel tanks, and when his aircraft was only a few feet in the air its motor stopped. He managed to bring the machine down abruptly a few feet short of a dolomite cliff. After settling his nerves and switching tanks he took off again and joined Brown and Hollick-Kenyon, who were circling in the other two Fokkers. The three machines reached Cambridge Bay without further incident and touched down on the ice beside the *Bay Maud*. The expedition's survivors, still weak from their ordeal, climbed gratefully into the Fokkers and were flown to Bathurst Inlet.

The trip back to civilization turned out to be nearly as exciting as the journey north. *En route* to Fort Reliance the pilots encoun-

tered fog and were forced to land on Musk Ox Lake. As they waited a snowstorm blew up. Quickly, they staked down the aircraft, then huddled inside the machines in their sleeping bags until the blizzard abated. Their next problem was to chop the aircraft skis free from the ice. The job took hours. Then, during his take-off run, Spence hit a snow drift and snapped one of the tubular support mounts for his engine. The damage was serious. Mechanics Tommy Siers and Graham Longley, who had accompanied the search aircraft, agreed to stay behind with Spence and repair the damaged Fairchild. The other aircraft continued south. But a section of one wing on Roy Brown's aircraft snapped. He was left behind while Cruickshank and the others flew on.

At Musk Ox Lake, Spence, Siers and Longley worked on the Fairchild in the finger-numbing cold. A frightful wind tore at their parkas. Snow and ice crystals stung their faces. They filed down the handles of several aluminum frying pans to repair the cracked motor mount. A tubular sleeve was taken from one of the interior fuselage stringers to replace the broken support tube. They had no fuel, so when the repairs were completed they tied the machine securely and built themselves a wind-break igloo to shelter their tent. By the fourth day they were almost out of food. To conserve strength they snuggled into their sleeping bags and waited. Spence shot an Arctic fox that strayed into the tent on the sixth day. It provided three days of good eating. On the morning of the twelfth day Andy Cruickshank arrived to pick them up. "I was never so glad to see anyone in my entire life!" Siers told a reporter later in Winnipeg. On the return trip south, Cruickshank stopped to rescue Roy Brown.

The mechanics had done an astonishing job at keeping the aircraft flying. They had been dubbed "the Black Gang" by Alan Bill of the *Winnipeg Tribune*. They had raised Cruickshank's Fokker after it had sunk

Opposite page: W.S. Tall, air engineer for Punch Dickins during his search for the MacAlpine expedition, 1929. (Provincial Archives of Manitoba, 1673)

through the ice at the mouth of the Burnside River. When the compressor struts had buckled on Spence's aircraft, they replaced them with the top of a radio mast. Innovation was the secret of survival in the north.

Siers, a master mechanic, who ended his career with Saskatchewan Government Airways at Prince Albert in the 1960s, was responsible for the development of the "oil dilution" system used by all piston-driven aircraft engines operating in cold climates around the world. Before Siers's brilliant discovery, hot engine oil had to be removed from the aircraft at the end of each winter working day before it turned to the consistency of tar. The oil was kept warm — usually inside a tent or building — until it was ready to use again. Siers's system did away with having to drain the oil. It allowed the pilot to inject aviation fuel into the engine oil to thin it, by using a toggle switch located inside the cockpit. In the morning, after the engine was heated and started, the aviation fuel burned off, leaving the oil to perform its normal function.

The MacAlpine expedition reached The Pas, Manitoba, in early December. A crowd gathered at the Malcrow Lake base to greet them as they climbed stiffly down from the yellow and blue Fokker. Despite their ordeal, all were in good health except Goodwin, who had to be carried to a taxi and taken to hospital, where three of his toes were amputated. When a reporter cornered Roy Brown for a statement on the epic flight and the heroism of those who took part in it, Roy told him modestly that he was overestimating the importance of what they did. "We were just doing our jobs. Flying is what we're paid to do. The only unusual thing about it is that we were flying up there at a time when we had no business being there."

The Coming of Age

From a practical standpoint the MacAlpine expedition had been little more than a succession of disasters. But it had demonstrated that men and aircraft could operate in the farthest reaches of the north and survive. It was hoped that these men and their aircraft could map a continent, save lives, discover minerals, shrink vast distances to provide goods and services to the remotest settlements and — ultimately — unite the nation in much the same way that the railroad had done fifty years before. Bush pilots and commercial operators pressed aircraft manufacturers to design machines that would make operations easier and safer.

Wop May introduced the first of the new breed of aircraft into the north when he purchased a Lockheed Vega. This high-wing

Fokker Universals base in Gold Pines, Ontario. September 1929. (Public Archives of Canada, PA 88798)

Right: Stan McMillan's smile and pipe became his trademarks throughout the north. The aircraft is a versatile Bellanca Pacemaker, which outperformed the larger Fokker Super Universals, making it the choice for many long-distance flights. McMillan's career safety record gave him the distinction of being one of the few pilots who never had to leave an aircraft behind in the bush. (Provincial Archives of Manitoba, 55)

Opposite page: (l to r) Vic Horner and Wop May kept ahead of their competition with the purchase of this new Lockheed Vega, first of its type in western Canada. (Provincial Archives of Alberta, 23)

Composite photograph promoting an Edmonton air show. (Provincial Archives of Alberta, 111)

monoplane with a range of 850 miles carried a pilot and six passengers and flew at 210 miles per hour. It was designed by Americans Jack Northrop and Allan Lougheed, who simplified his company's name to Lockheed. The Vega was a delight to fly after the unheated Fairchilds and Fokkers.

Aviation records were being broken every month. Doc Oaks and Pat Reid made the inaugural northern commercial flight to Richmond Gulf on Hudson Bay; Punch Dickins became the first to reach the Arctic port of Aklavik; Stan McMillan flew the first aircraft to Herschel Island in the Arctic Ocean. Leigh Brintnell and John Hunter completed a survey flight in a Fokker trimotor from Winnipeg to Aklavik, then flew over the Mackenzie Mountains to Dawson City in the Yukon, from there to Prince Rupert on the Pacific Ocean, then back to Winnipeg. Wop May and Vic Horner opened a non-stop mail service between Winnipeg and Edmonton.

The discovery of mineral wealth in the far north made Edmonton, the country's most northern major city, a springboard for all prospecting and mining development. The city led the country in shipments of air freight. Its airport facilities were expanded to accommodate the increase in traffic. Finally, early in 1929, after much discussion, the government agreed to test a northern airmail service. Commercial radio stations broadcast the news of the experimental mail delivery to northern communities. Punch Dickins, with engineer Lew Parmenter and postal inspector Tom Reilley, took off in a Fokker Super Universal on the first mail run. In every community across the north, inhabitants came out to meet them for their mail. At Fort Simpson people grabbed the mail-bags, tossed them onto a dog sled and mushed off to make the delivery. At Fort Resolution there was a short delay when Dickins hit an ice hummock on take-off, breaking a ski strut and bending the Fokker's metal propeller as the aircraft nosed over.

As they had brought no spare parts, Dickins used whatever he could find to repair the plane. A water pipe, an offering from the local priest, was used to repair the undercarriage strut. Straightening the propeller took more time. Dickins and Parmenter managed to bend one blade back into position but the other was too badly scrolled at the tip to straighten. When they tried, the end snapped off. Dickins took a hacksaw to the good blade so that it would match the broken one. It worked like a charm, with barely any vibration. The Fokker made a smooth take-off and continued the mail deliveries. On the return journey Dickins brought a load of furs to Winnipeg. The furs reached the wholesale market in four days instead of the usual four months.

Above: Western Canada Airways pilots Punch Dickins and Lew Parmenter in a Fokker Super Universal prepare to take off from Fort McMurray to Fort Simpson to open the first mail run. (Provincial Archives of Manitoba, 572)

Below: Arrival of Fokker Super Universal at Fort Simpson. Punch Dickins stands in the cockpit. (Public Archives of Canada, C 57672)

Federal politics played a part in the final decision to begin the northern airmail service. Later that year, when the remote northern communities of the Mackenzie River district began to receive their Christmas mail, it was delivered by the politically acceptable Commercial Airways and not an apolitical Punch Dickins, the man who had spent years of hard work convincing postal officials they should have a northern airmail service.

The New York stock-market crash of 1929 caused the collapse of Canada's financial markets. Hundreds of thousands of Canadian investors lost enormous sums of money. The resulting financial chaos devastated commercial aviation. Venture capital for northern mining development all but disappeared. Everybody searched for scapegoats. Some criminal charges were laid.

Isaac Solloway, of the brokerage firm Solloway, Mills & Company Ltd., had been one of the principal backers of aviation in Alberta. He was accused of causing the collapse of Alberta oil stock in the market. He and his partner, Harvey Mills, were arrested. Solloway's firm had financed Commercial Airways, and Solloway had enthusiastically served as its first president. Within days after Alberta's Premier James Brownlee had praised Solloway for financing Wop May's historic first airmail flight from Edmonton to Aklavik, the government charged Solloway with fraud. He was convicted and sentenced to four months in prison.

Before he was sentenced, Solloway closed his chain of brokerage offices, leaving Commercial Airways teetering on the brink of bankruptcy. Wop May, with Solloway's backing, had bought new aircraft to service the lucrative mail contracts the company had won from Punch Dickins. With Solloway gone the company's line of credit was cancelled by the bank. Reluctantly, Com-

Avro Avian of Western Canada Airways on the Assiniboine River, 1929. (Public Archives of Canada, C 59957)

mercial Airways merged with its major competitor, Canadian Airways Limited. This firm, formerly Western Canada Airways, was an amalgamation of several smaller firms that extended across Canada. For a logo it adopted the image of a flying Canada goose. Canadian Airways Limited (CAL) opened a new flying-boat service between Victoria and Vancouver on the west coast. Don MacLaren was put in charge of the operation. Wop May, Archie McMullen, engineer Horace Torrie and other Commercial Airways staff joined the expanding company.

CAL transported passengers, mail and freight. As well, the company received a contract to dust calcium arsenate over a caterpillar infestation that had struck the trees in Vancouver's Stanley Park, threatening to turn it into a wasteland. To spread the insect poison, each flying-boat was outfitted with a storage bin behind the cockpit. At the bottom of the bin, trap doors were installed on either side of the fuselage that could be opened by the pilot in flight. Operations were conducted from a scow anchored in English Bay; from there the dust bags were opened and loaded into the aircraft cargo bins. The work began at dawn and continued until the sea breeze began to blow the dust beyond the target area.

A former boxer, Norm Forrester, flew one of the three Boeing flying-boats on the operation: "I can remember flying about one hundred feet above the trees behind and to the left of the lead plane. The air was so calm that on the return run I could see the first dust swath still settling into the trees." In minutes layers of dead caterpillars covered the park. (Years later, Forrester was still remembered as the man who helped save Stanley Park.)

Meanwhile, in the north, James Richardson placed Punch Dickins in charge of the

Captain Wop May, chief pilot of Canadian Airways (r), and E. W. Stull, mechanic, with Junkers W34. (Public Archives of Canada, C 23486)

Right: Junkers W34 and Bellanca Pacemaker of Canadian Airways Ltd., Contact Lake, Northwest Territories, 1933. (Public Archives of Canada, C 25139)

Opposite page: Junkers W34 of Canadian Airways Ltd., 1935. (Public Archives of Canada, C 57531)

Below: Junkers W34 at Carcross, Yukon, in front of the stern-wheeler *S.S. Tutski.* (Public Archives of Canada, PA 88683)

Left: Jack Moar tying up to take on a load of calcium arsenate dust to control an outbreak of tent caterpillars at Stanley Park, Vancouver, British Columbia, 1929. (Provincial Archives of Manitoba, 56)

expanding Mackenzie River District, which had been serviced by the now defunct Commercial Airways. It seemed only right that Dickins, who had developed northern airmail in the first place, should end up with not only the mail contract, but the district's freight and passengers services, which had been provided by competitor Isaac Solloway. If he felt any sense of achievement from fortune's turn of events or from May's sell-out of the company to CAL he never spoke of it. CAL's attention had turned to more ambitious projects than carrying the mail. A huge

Below: DeHavilland 83 "Fox Moth." Airmail delivery for northern Saskatchewan at the Prince Albert base of Canadian Airways Ltd. (Public Archives of Canada, PA 8891)

Commercial Airways Limited
HEAD OFFICE: EDMONTON
BASES SHOWN ON MAP LEGEND

MACKENZIE RIVER DISTRICT

RATES

From Fort McMurray To—	Passenger	Express Per Lb.
Fort Chipewyan	$ 35.00	$ .20
Fort Fitzgerald	65.00	.35
Fort Smith	65.00	.35
Fort Resolution	100.00	.70
Hay River	135.00	.75
Fort Providence	160.00	.85
Fort Simpson	205.00	1.00
Fort Wrigley	240.00	1.3
Fort Norman	280.00	1.65
Good Hope	325.00	2.15
Arctic Red River	375.00	2.50
Fort McPherson	390.00	2.60
Aklavik	410.00	2.70

The above are the rates for ordinary schedule flights on the route mentioned.

Special flights may be arranged for.

Each passenger is entitled to carry 25 lbs. of baggage free, all in excess of that weight charged accordingly.

All traffic rates listed above are subject to change without notice.

MAP OF
Air Lines to the Arctic
OPERATED BY
Commercial Airways
LIMITED

POINTS of CALL
AGENCIES
AIR BASES

WINTER SCHEDULE
1929 - 1930

NORTH-BOUND
Leave Fort McMurray
For Fort Resolution:
Nov. 27; Dec. 4, 11, 18, 25;
Jan. 1, 8, 15, 22, 29;
Feb. 5, 12, 19, 26;
Mar. 5, 12, 19, 26; Apr. 2, 9.
For Fort Simpson:
Nov. 27; Dec. 25; Jan. 22;
Feb. 12; Mar. 5, 26.
For Aklavik:
Nov. 27; Jan. 22; Mar. 26.

SOUTH-BOUND
Leave Aklavik:
Dec. 3; Feb. 28; Apr. 1.
Leave Fort Simpson:
Dec. 5, 28; Jan. 28; Feb. 15;
Mar. 8; Apr. 3.
Leave Fort Resolution:
Nov. 29; Dec. 6, 13, 20, 28;
Jan. 3, 10, 17, 24;
Feb. 1, 7, 15, 21, 28;
Mar. 8, 14, 21, 28; Apr. 4, 11.

On the above flights, the aircraft will stop at intermediate posts.

The schedule is tentative, and rigid adherence to it will depend upon weather.

SHIPPING INSTRUCTIONS:

Mark North-bound Parcels care of "COMMERCIAL AIRWAYS LIMITED, FORT McMURRAY, Alberta," via Northern Alberta Railways' Express—"Air charges COLLECT" or "PREPAID."

Shippers are required to prepay Railway Express Charges to Fort McMurray on North Bound Traffic.

EXAMPLE:

From	JOHN DOE, 411 - 81st Ave., Edmonton, Alta.
To	JAS SMITH, Ft. Resolution, N.W.T., c/o Commercial Airways Ltd., Ft. McMurray, Alta.

Via N. A. R. Express.   "Air Charges Collect" (or otherwise)

Pack parcels securely. Parcels must be kept within the following limit (outside measurements) 12-in. x 20-in. x 60-in.

Add 2-in. to width for each decrease of 12-in. in length.

C. BECKER, General Manager.

uranium deposit had been discovered at Great Bear Lake by prospector Gilbert La-Bine.

LaBine, a prospector with Eldorado Gold Mines Limited, had flown with Leigh Brintnell a year earlier in a Fokker Super Universal to investigate a report of minerals along the shores of Great Bear Lake. Brintnell dropped LaBine and his supplies at Echo Bay, fifty miles south of the Arctic Circle. From there LaBine staked his claims. His prime interest was gold, and the need to find a new resource base for his company. Eldorado's ore reserves at its northern Mani-

toba mining operations were no longer profitable. When LaBine finished staking his claims, Punch Dickins flew him back to civilization.

In the spring of 1930, shortly before breakup, LaBine again flew to Great Bear Lake, this time with mining engineer Charles St. Paul. Hauling their supply sleds in freezing surface water that at times reached their knees, they crossed the ice on Echo Bay and made a camp on the shore. During their second trip for supplies, St. Paul suffered snow blindness from the intense glare of the sun reflected off the snow and ice. For several days he remained immobilized at camp, shielded from any light and with a poultice of wet tea leaves covering his eyes. While St. Paul recovered, LaBine went prospecting. Close to the camp he discovered a vein of silver ore. It ended abruptly at a bluff, where LaBine chipped off a chunk

Opposite page: Airline schedule of Commercial Airways Ltd. for the Mackenzie District. (Private Collection)

Below: Inexperience on glassy-water landing resulted in the wiping out of this new Fairchild 71 at Lac La Ronge, Saskatchewan. (Public Archives of Canada, PA 98915)

Prospectors Gilbert LaBine (l) and Spud Arsenault (r) examine pitchblende samples from the Eldorado Mine at Great Bear Lake, 1931. (Provincial Archives of Alberta, 66.122/19a)

Refuelling Archie McMullen's Bellanca Pacemaker at Eldorado Mine, N.W.T. (l to r) Eric Johnson, Casey van der Linden, August 1931. (Public Archives of Canada, PA 14748)

of black rock, which he brought back to camp. Inside the darkened shack where St. Paul lay, LaBine noticed that the black rock gave off a subdued and eerie phosphorescent glow. His hands trembled as he recognized what he had discovered: pitchblende. He said nothing to St. Paul but hurried back to the spot at the bluff and hammered off several more specimens with the black, bubbled surface of pitchblende. When St. Paul recovered the use of his eyes, LaBine presented him with their find.

By the following year, some four thousand claims had been staked along the shores of Great Bear Lake. Bush camps were springing up like spring mushrooms. The area was a warehouse of mineral deposits: silver, copper, cobalt, manganese and pitchblende. Fortuitously, a coal deposit was discovered on the northwestern side of Great Bear Lake, so there was no shortage of fuel to operate and heat the hundreds of mining camps. Although LaBine had found

a fortune in ore, he needed money to extract it from the ground. In 1931 no financier was interested in mine investments near the Arctic Circle, a thousand miles from the nearest rail line, on the shore of an inaccessible lake that was frozen ten months of the year. With the world economy in chaos from the Great Depression, few investors were interested in gambling on mining properties. LaBine kept trying.

The first commercial flights to Great Bear Lake began in 1931. Punch Dickins and Walter Gilbert brought in most of the pioneers and their equipment and supplies. The region had never been properly mapped or surveyed. Dickins and Gilbert's hand-drawn maps, sketched during their travels, soon became the recognized naviga-

(l to r) Lewis Parmenter, Col. Charles A. Lindburgh, and W.E. Gilbert during Lindburgh's stopover at Aklavik on his way to the Orient via Alaska with his wife, Anne Morrow. (Provincial Archives of Manitoba, 1531)

tional guides for all pilots operating throughout the area. (In the United States, Captain Elrey Borge Jeppesen, an ex-barnstormer working with Boeing Air Transport, later part of United Air Lines, was also making notes and drawing maps of the airports, letdown procedures and air routes that he travelled between Chicago and Oakland, California. His notebooks became the basis for the Jeppesen Airway Manual, used throughout the world.)

Gilbert had become an expert in navigational plotting in 1930, when the Canadian government chartered a Fokker seaplane from Western Canada Airways for a scientific expedition into the Arctic. Gilbert plotted the lines of magnetic variation and angles of compass declination. He circumnavigated King William Island and investigated the remains of the Sir John Franklin Expedition of 1845-48. The project turned out to be a great success and did much to develop geographical knowledge of the Canadian Arctic. (In 1933 Gilbert won the McKee Trophy for his contribution to Canadian aviation.)

In 1931 Gilbert bunked in at the first camp of what would eventually become Port Radium. "It had only a few tents, and we slept on ice-covered spruce boughs. Dry firewood was scarce, and the damp logs hardly gave off any heat. In the morning it was so cold that my beard, frozen by the congealed moisture from my breath, had to be pulled loose from the sleeping bag's blanket hood."

In summer flotillas of strange craft sailed down the Mackenzie River to the Arctic, carrying the entire spectrum of humanity. This wasn't like other gold rushes. There was no Dawson City at the end of the trail; there were no bars, no dance hall girls and no fights. There was only the same desolation and empty landscape all the way to the shore of the Arctic Ocean. There were desperate farmers whose drought-stricken crops had failed and who set out by raft seeking their personal Eldorado. City dwellers without jobs pulled up stakes and sailed north. From the drought districts of the Peace River people joined the trek in caravans and covered wagons. A family in a rough-hewn scow powered by a home-made paddle-wheel and carrying two white mules and a truck made it as far as Fort Norman where turbulent rapids halted their journey. They disembarked. Local Indians ignored the spectacle of the first motor vehicle in the settlement to gather in wonder and examine the albino mules. The family decided to abandon the journey and opened the area's first motorized-transport freight business.

The economic situation grew worse. The Depression spread like an epidemic. Businesses failed. Grain prices dropped to record lows. Canadian air transportation suffered a blow when, as an economy measure, the federal government, under Conservative Prime Minister R.B. Bennett, cancelled all airmail contracts. When the news broke, all aviation-industry salaries were reduced by 10 per cent. Pilots left for other jobs. F. Roy Brown left CAL to form his own company, Wings Limited. Yet in spite of economic setbacks, CAL continued to expand its freight and passenger services on the west

Fokker and WACO aircraft of Wings Ltd. at Lac du Bonnet, Manitoba, 1934. (Public Archives of Canada, PA 103441)

Above: The arrival in Edmonton of the new Mackenzie Air Services Bellanca from the United States draws a crowd in spite of the cold. (Provincial Archives of Alberta, 79.128)

Below: A matter of cargo priority, 1936. (Public Archives of Canada, C 61798)

coast. Even without funds for mining, business along the Mackenzie River grew. When control of provincial natural resources was handed to the prairie provinces by Ottawa, CAL took over the federal government's forestry patrols from the air force.

Because of the Depression, the RCAF came into direct competition with private enterprise. The air force's Civil Operations Branch provided the federal government with personnel and equipment transport, and in several instances took business away from established commercial companies desperate for business. James Richardson used his considerable political influence to put a stop to these unfair competitive practices. In addition, he persuaded the prime minister to restore northern airmail delivery.

Since there was little in the way of operating cash, most business transactions in the north were based on a system of barter.

Bush pilots dealt with prospectors, trappers, Indians, Eskimos, Métis, police, woodcutters and traders. There were no banks, so few people carried cash. On one trip Punch Dickins's revenues amounted to $240 worth of wolf bounties, cured fur pelts from four hundred muskrats, two red foxes, seven martens, five mink, one lynx and fifteen dollars in cash.

The Eskimos loved flying. On a trip to Aklavik one of them asked Dickins if he would trade his airplane. Dickins offered to hand it over for a thousand white fox pelts — worth about $20,000 in 1932. The Eskimo thought it over and decided it was a good deal. When Dickins asked how he planned

Pilot Archie McMullen (second left) is met by his customers at Coppermine, 1933. (Provincial Archives of Alberta, A5853)

Indian woman of the Northwest Territories, with pipe.
(Z.L. Leigh Collection)

to fly it , the man replied confidently: "You fly him. I fly him."

Most Indians, on the other hand, were reluctant to be taken aloft. Dickins, who was known to the Indians as "Thunder Bird," once persuaded an Indian at Fort Resolution to guide him by air to a prospector's camp. The man agreed provided Dickins tied a heavy rope around his waist to keep him from falling out of the aircraft.

The first fatal bush-flying accident occurred when a Fokker Super Universal, flown by Andy Cruickshank, crashed into a steep, heavily treed hill after leaving Cameron Bay for Fort Rae on Great Bear Lake. Cruickshank, who had played an important role in rescuing the MacAlpine expedition, was one of the north's most experienced pilots. Con Farrell reported the wreckage of the blue and yellow Fokker. Next day Farrell and Walter Gilbert reached the site and found Cruickshank's body and the bodies of his two mechanics, Harry King and Horace Torrie. It was thought that, while airborne, a cylinder head had broken loose and smashed into the cockpit.

Above: Fairchild 71 with
wings folded in a snow
hangar at Port Harrison,
1933. (Provincial
Archives of Manitoba,
265)

Left: C.H. (Punch)
Dickins, bush pilot, 1933.
(Provincial Archives of
Manitoba, 1494)

Cruickshank, a former RCMP officer, had spent most of his working life in the north. He loved the people who lived there and the endless contest for survival against the elements.

Two other veteran flyers, Paul Calder and his engineer, Bill Nadin, died when their Fairchild crashed in a blizzard between Fort Rae and Great Bear Lake. Shortly before his death, Calder had told his father, an Edmonton city alderman: "If it comes, I hope it comes quickly." His burned body was found in the charred wreckage of his airplane by Wop May.

The tiny community of Fort McMurray, at the junction of the Peace and Athabasca rivers, became, because of its railhead, the gateway to northern development. Enormous amounts of equipment and mining supplies destined for the mineral fields around Great Bear Lake funnelled through the settlement. Within months Fort McMurray became the largest commercial air base in Canada. Numbers of Canadian Airways pilots, engineers and ground-support personnel made their home in this isolated community. Walter Gilbert arrived in a snowstorm with his wife, Jeanne, British Columbia's first woman pilot. They landed, collected their bags and waded through the

Right: Bush pilots Archie McMullen (l) and Con Farrell (r). (City of Edmonton Archives, A81-276)

Previous page: Competitors at Cameron Bay, Great Bear Lake, February 1933. One Fokker is owned by CAL; the other, flown by Z.L. Leigh, belongs to Explorers Air Transport. (Z.L. Leigh Collection)

Previous page inset: Wop May with load of Eskimo furs for the south. Unlike the area's native Indians, the Eskimos loved airplanes and flying. (Provincial Archives of Manitoba, 222)

knee-deep snow to check into the Franklin, the only commercial hotel for five hundred miles in any direction. It was owned by an Irish couple by the name of O'Coffey who charged their guests whatever the market would bear. The Franklin had the luxury of a fireplace in every room. Later, to save money, the Gilberts moved into a two-room shack behind the hotel. Paul Calder scrounged an iron bath-tub for the couple, and neighbours provided them with a few sticks of furniture. What essentials they lacked were ordered through the Eaton's mail-order catalogue and delivered by rail. Jeanne learned to cook on a wood stove.

Violet May, Wop's wife, lived close by. A former champion equestrian and polo player, Violet owned a radio, which provided the wives with entertainment from the outside world while their husbands were away. An Edmonton radio station carried a folksy program titled "Hello to the North," which gave residents of northern communities within broadcast range a method of exchanging messages with friends and relatives in the south. To pass the time and ease their isolation, people in the northern towns and settlements played bridge, visited each other and organized outdoor sports activities. Ressa McMullen, whose husband, Archie,

Left: Stanley Neil Knight, aircraft engineer, and W.E. Gilbert, pilot, on their trip to the north magnetic pole. (Provincial Archives of Manitoba, 524-1)

Opposite page: Remains of a Fairchild from Fort Chipewyan being dragged by sleigh to Fort McMurray for repairs. (Public Archives of Canada, C 57765)

was a CAL pilot at Fort McMurray, learned how to handle a dog team. She became a first-class shot, and managed to keep herself and the other wives well stocked with moose meat. An unheated shack provided freezer storage to the town during winter months.

Fort McMurray wives often missed their husbands at Christmastime, when bad weather might delay them or when mail delivery fell on the holiday. Con Farrell spent so many Christmases away from home he became known as the Santa Claus of the Mackenzie. One holiday season he flew a missionary's wife and new baby from Aklavik to Coppermine, where they choked down a Christmas dinner of raw fish and seal blub-

ber with local Eskimos. Another Christmas, Farrell flew out to find a trapper who had fallen through the ice with his dogs and furs. The poor man managed to claw his way out of the freezing water and reach his cabin. Farrell found him on Christmas Day and flew him to Fort Reliance. The next Christmas, Farrell saved a group of reindeer herdsmen who had been lost in a blizzard after their animals stampeded.

There were many economic advantages to living in the north in the 1930s. Although southern economies faltered and collapsed and people lost their jobs, northerners could always find work of some sort. Farmers who had abandoned their drought-stricken land marvelled at the green forests and unlimited water in the north. Even in slack periods, when CAL laid off some of its junior personnel, there was always work to do. When McMullen was grounded temporarily, he kept himself busy by cutting and hauling cord wood for the townspeople. When summer came, residents grew vegetables, built a tennis court out of plywood and held picnics for the children. A few, prepared to brave the periodic swarms of blackflies and mosquitoes, worked on their sun tans.

Albert Johnson was a short, wiry, forty-year-old drifter who rafted down the Peel River to Fort McPherson in the summer of 1931. He owned neither a gun nor any supplies. But he did have an enormous amount of money tucked into his pockets, in small tight rolls. He had also a vicious temper, and he pre-

ferred his own company. Johnson built a small log cabin near the Rat River, then bought himself an arsenal of guns and ammunition from William Douglas, the local Hudson's Bay factor. Soon after, local Indian trappers discovered that he had been tampering with their trap lines, replacing their traps with his. When confronted with his duplicity Johnson threatened to shoot them.

Wop May heard about Johnson from local RCMP officers during one of his regular mail flights between Fort McMurray and Aklavik. His sympathies lay entirely with the Indians. "Why don't you arrest the bugger?" May demanded of the police in Aklavik. RCMP Inspector Alexander Eames promised action and assigned officer Edgar Millen, a Belfast-born constable, to investigate. Millen, Constable Alfred King and trapper Joe Bernard harnessed their dog teams and

mushed out to Johnson's cabin, some sixty-five miles from their detachment at Arctic Red River.

The patrol reached the cabin at night. The structure, built of heavy logs with gun slits cut through its walls, resembled an old frontier fort. The trio approached cautiously, noticing no foot tracks in the snow around the squat blockhouse. King pounded on the door several times, but there was no reply nor were there any sounds from inside the cabin. The Mounties left for Aklavik to obtain a search warrant. A week later, on New Year's Eve, Constable King returned to Johnson's fort, accompanied by another constable, Bert McDowall. After hammering on the door King threatened in a loud voice to chop it down with an axe. There was still no response from inside the fort. As King

raised his axe, a bullet ripped through the door and struck him two inches below the heart, shattering his ribs. McDowall fired with his service revolver as King, trailing blood across the snow, crawled away from the line of fire. Swiftly, McDowall lifted the injured man over his shoulder and carried him to cover at a nearby river bank, where he wrapped him in blankets then strapped him to the sled.

With a crack of the whip the exhausted sleigh dogs were mushed back to Aklavik and the Mission Hospital. The trip took twenty hours in a temperature of -42°C. King survived the agonizing journey and

The RCMP officers who hunted down Albert Johnson, the mad trapper of Rat River. (City of Edmonton Archives, 15)

made a remarkable recovery. Inspector Eames placed a broadcast over the Royal Canadian Signal Corps' radio station, the Voice of the Northern Lights, asking listeners throughout the Mackenzie Delta area to assist in the capture of Albert Johnson. Within the week a posse of well-armed civilian volunteers, RCMP constables and Indian guides were encircling the cabin.

Eames felt confident they had trapped their man. He ordered Johnson out of the log fort. The mad trapper opened fire. The police fired back. After several volleys were exchanged, Eames instructed his men to storm the door. Crouching low, Millen and McDowall raced in and began pounding at it with their rifle butts, but Johnson's firing forced them back. Millen, who had caught a glimpse of the fort's smoke-filled interior, reported that Johnson had dug himself a manhole below the line of fire. Eames decided to wear his quarry down. He would wait until early the following day before attacking again. The men bedded down for the night.

Next morning, under Eames's direction, Joe Verville crept forward with a bundle of dynamite. When he was within range he lit the fuse and hurled the package against the door, which exploded in a shower of splintered wood and flames. Part of the roof collapsed. The men fired several volleys into the smouldering cabin. After the smoke had cleared, Eames signalled his men forward in the eerie silence. Johnson lay motionless, sprawled face down on the floor. The lawmen relaxed. Then, suddenly, Johnson reached for his rifle and fired into the group. The surprised attackers ran for cover.

Furious, Eames organized another attack, this time using a heavier charge of dynamite. A second mighty explosion erupted, leaving a huge cloud hanging over the blackened ruin of what had once been Johnson's blockhouse. Satisfied that their fugitive had died in the explosion, the men charged. They probed the darkness with flashlights looking for a body. Shots erupted from behind the splintered logs. A bullet tore through Eames's hat. Karl Garlund, a trapper holding a flashlight, had his hand shattered by another bullet. Johnson was obviously a lunatic. He seemed to be invincible. Eames decided to leave two men to guard the ruined fort and return to Aklavik for more men and supplies.

Within five days Eames had gathered another posse, more ammunition and more supplies, including a stink bomb developed by Earl Hersey, a staff sergeant with the Signals Corps. The party reinforcements raced back over the hard-packed snow. The two guards reported no movement from inside the shattered fort. The inspector decided to attack immediately. The men crept forward and entered the cabin. Inside they found a scattering of provisions on the floor, dozens of spent cartridges but no sign of their quarry. In one corner of the double-walled ruin they found the manhole where Johnson had crouched in safety during the explosions. Behind the cabin they uncovered a food cache hidden in a tree. The fugitive had flown the coop. Disgusted, Eames left Millen and the main party to continue the search while he returned to Aklavik.

For the next two weeks Johnson played games with his trackers, skilfully out-manoeuvring them at every turn. He travelled up creek beds where there was no snow to leave a trail, then walked in ever widening circles until he seemed to vanish. He wore his snow-shoes backwards to confuse his pursuers. In the late afternoon of the eleventh day of the search, Sergeant Robert Riddell sighted smoke rising from a ravine. He signalled Millen and the others to join him. Silently the group edged closer. Below the lip of the ravine they sighted a solitary man hunched over a small cooking fire. Millen sent two men down the bank with instructions to work their way in behind an uprooted tree that lay a few feet from the fire, while he and Riddell attacked from the front. However, before they managed to climb down the rocky slope, Johnson heard them and dived behind the fallen tree, using its roots as a barricade.

In the fading light Garlund saw the fugitive's dark outline against the snow. He took careful aim and then fired. Johnson fell forward as if he had been hit. The Mounties remained crouched, watching and waiting for any sign of life from the inert form lying on the snow. After a two-hour wait with faces numb from the cold, Millen whispered to Riddell that they should attack. Cautiously, they crunched through the deep snow towards the fallen tree. As they approached, Riddell caught sight of a rifle barrel inching its way through the roots. He shouted a warning to Millen and jumped behind a tree for cover. Johnson fired. The bullet nicked the bark and grazed Millen's check. Millen aimed his rifle at Johnson and pulled the trigger. The rifle jammed. Before he could scramble out of the line of fire, Johnson shot him.

At first light Sergeant Hersey crawled to Millen's cold corpse, then worked his way to the fallen tree. He stood and waved to the others. Johnson had escaped. Riddell tied Millen's body to his sled and set out for Aklavik. Inspector Eames raged at the turn of events. A single demented fugitive had murdered and outsmarted the best men he had sent out against him — not once, but twice. Eames appealed for volunteers over the radio. Men with dog teams from throughout the district answered the call. National newspapers picked up the story and headlined their front pages with stories about the Mad Trapper.

Within days Eames had enough manpower to run his quarry to ground. His next problem was logistics. Johnson was travelling solo, living off the land and carrying little to slow him down, while his pursuers needed large amounts of supplies in order to cover the long distances required for their pursuit. Providing men and dogs with sufficient food to stay on the trail for several weeks would slow the search. Johnson might slip away a third time. Eames made up his mind to use aircraft to keep his trackers supplied as they fanned out across the country. He would start an air search to find Johnson.

Until the Royal Canadian Mounted Police formed its own aviation branch in 1937, Canadian federal police officers depended on bush pilots and the RCAF to cover the sparsely inhabited north. Flying with local Mounties, pilots checked for illegal hunting, fishing and fur trapping, and occasionally took part in criminal investigations. Early in February, Eames wired the new Canadian Airways superintendent, Punch Dickins, in Edmonton, requesting air support. Dickins flew Constable Carter, Millen's replacement, into Fort McMurray the next day. Dickins gave Wop May the assignment of supplying Eames's force and trying to locate Johnson from the air. May left in a Bellanca Pacemaker with Constable Carter and engineer Jack Bowen. A snowstorm forced them to land, and they spent the night at Fort Smith. Next day, although the weather remained poor, they managed to reach Arctic Red River, where a message from Eames awaited May. The plane was ordered to meet the searchers at the junction of the Rat and Peel rivers.

May took off and searched the area for several hours without seeing any sign of life below. He decided to continue on to Aklavik. That night another snowstorm almost buried the Bellanca. It took several hours to dig the machine out. The search resumed. Dr. Urquhart, the physician who had treated Constable King and who possessed a pair of keen eyes, joined those on board the aircraft. As the aircraft circled the V-shaped junction of the two rivers, Jack Bowen spotted the four-man patrol waving at the Bellanca. May dropped his supplies and passengers and flew on with Bowen.

Flying low and using a pair of field glasses they sighted a single snow-shoe trail and followed the tracks for several miles up the Barrier River. It appeared that Johnson had doubled back on his tracks. A new trail led away from the river to the west, towards the mountain ranges that divided the Yukon from Alaska.

May and Bowen landed at the base camp and reported to Eames. It was decided to shift their operation closer to the mountains and establish several pursuit patrols, each of which would be supplied by the Bellanca. In the days that followed, May spent his time ferrying food supplies, sleds, dogs, ammunition and personnel between the patrol areas. But bad weather cut down the number of available hours for the ground patrols and aerial surveillance. The artful Johnson used caribou tracks to cover his trail, and for a while the patrols lost him. Trappers finally picked up his trail, which led to the Bell Pass into Alaska. They noticed that Johnson appeared to be taking more rest breaks and covering less ground. Above the tree line there was no kindling, so Johnson couldn't make a fire to cook, to melt snow for drinking water or to keep warm.

When the weather cleared again, May and Bowen rejoined the RCMP patrols. Flying with Riddell and Eames, May headed for La Pierre House near the place where local trappers had reported seeing Johnson's tracks. A morning fog delayed May's take-off next day, but by late afternoon he caught up with the quarry. He followed Johnson's snow-shoe trail to where it disappeared abruptly near the fork of the Eagle and Bell rivers. May reported his findings to the ground patrols. Far down the Eagle River the Mounties picked up the trail. They broke into smaller groups and fanned out along the river banks. The Bellanca flew cover ahead of the patrols, following the river's twisted course through the empty, silent wilderness. Suddenly, May spotted a man in the centre of the river. He banked the aircraft for a better view and saw one of the patrols encircling the lone figure.

Hersey's patrol had come upon Johnson quite suddenly as he was backtracking to cover his trail. Hersey grabbed a rifle from his sled and fired. Johnson kneeled, unfastened his snow-shoes and ran to the river bank for cover. He tried to claw his way up the steep slope. As Hersey moved in, Johnson turned suddenly and squeezed off two quick shots. Hersey dropped with a cry and lay twitching in the snow, bullets in his knee and lung.

Inside the Bellanca, May and Bowen saw the distinct puffs of smoke and fire flashes from the muzzles of the rifles below them. They saw a single figure collapse on the snow below. Was it Johnson or one of the Mounties? The Bellanca circled.

Other patrol members moved up swiftly, their fire pinning Johnson down as he tried to cross the river. He burrowed into the snow. Using his pack for a rifle rest, he returned the lawmen's fire. The officers hesitated, calling for him to surrender. But Johnson kept firing. He had no intention of being taken alive. Then, from every position, the Mounties opened fire. Bullets ripped into Johnson's legs, hip and shoulders. Finally, one of the shots shattered his spine.

May and Bowen made a low-level pass and saw Johnson lying face-down in the snow still clutching his rifle. May waggled his wings to signal the other trackers that their pursuit was over. He landed the Bellanca in a cloud of deep, powdery snow close to the wounded Hersey, then scrambled out with Bowen and waded through hip-deep snow to join Riddell, who was attending to Hersey's wounds. The flyers examined Johnson's body. The emaciated twisted face of the corpse seemed to be frozen in a terrible grimace of ironic laughter. The gaping mouth and surrounding matted beard gave May and Bowen the impression of some wild animal. A tin can tied around Johnson's

The surest form of northern transport. (Provincial Archives of Alberta, 79.128)

neck was stuffed with US and Canadian currency plus a number of gold teeth. The Mounties loaded Hersey gently into the Bellanca. It took the men an hour to tramp down a runway in the snow before May could attempt a take-off. At the Aklavik hospital Dr. Urquhart operated on Hersey's torn lung. He removed a bullet just under the skin on the sergeant's back and told Hersey that without the air rescue he would not have survived. May's final act in the saga was to fly Edgar Millen's body to Edmonton for burial. As for the incredibly resilient Albert Johnson — if that was his real name — no one ever discovered who he was, where he came from, why he happened to be such a superb marksman or how be came to be carrying so much money and someone else's gold fillings. A number of claims to his estate were filed by people claiming to be relatives in Canada and the United States. None could be verified. The true identity of the Mad Trapper of Rat River remains a mystery.

Growing Pains

Throughout the lean years of the 1930s, northern mining developments sustained Canadian bush pilots and allowed the aviation industry to survive and grow. Canadian Airways Limited was the largest and most successful of the big companies; even during the Depression, it continued to expand. Discoveries of gold in the provinces of British Columbia, Manitoba, Ontario and Quebec provided flurries of intense local interest. There were legends about such men as Jules Timmins, Sir Harry Oakes and others who made incredible fortunes from gold exploration. Farther north, in the Territories, the main action centred on Great Bear Lake and Gilbert LaBine's discovery of pitchblende on behalf of Eldorado Mining and Exploration.

Most of the world's radium derived

Bellanca 66-70 Air Cruiser of Mackenzie Air Service Ltd. taking off from LaBine Point, Northwest Territories, August 1937. (Public Archives of Canada, PA 1481)

from pitchblende came from a remote copper mine in the Belgian Congo owned by King Leopold and priced at a mind-boggling $70,000 per gram. The radium taken from the pitchblende at LaBine Point on Great Bear Lake had assayed out to be much higher than that of the Congo. La-Bine's find also contained appreciable quantities of silver.

Eldorado's problem was not getting the ore out but bringing in the mining equipment and supplies over a tortuous water route that was open only a few months of the year. The river systems of the Mackenzie and Athabasca flowed through a formidable series of rapids, swamps, muskeg and mountains. From where the railway ended, at Fort McMurray, everything had to be shipped north along the river routes for fifteen hundred miles. The logistics involved for Eldorado were formidable. Nevertheless, LaBine persevered in his quest for development funds. The world's acute uranium shortage proved to be the lure that brought in private investors.

When radiologist and surgeon Howard Atwood Kelly of Baltimore's Johns Hopkins Hospital heard about LaBine's discovery, he understood immediately that LaBine could break the Belgian monopoly. The scientific and medical community needed LaBine's radium. Encouraged by Dr. Kelly, LaBine enlisted the aid of a French scientist, Marcel Pochon, a former colleague of Pierre and Marie Curie, the discoverers of radium. Pochon had been squeezing minuscule amounts of uranium from a deposit in Cornwall. He added his encouragement and technical advice to the project.

With first financing in place, LaBine shipped a compressor, a chain fall and hydraulic hoisting equipment, diesel engines and an assortment of other supplies by rail, river and lakes to his mine site at La-Bine Point. The next problem was to find an inexpensive method of refining the pitchblende, which required six tons of chemicals to treat approximately one ton of concentrate. Pochon suggested shipping the pitchblende to a refinery in the south instead of trying to move tons of chemicals north. It made sense. A short time later, a chance meeting between LaBine and his friend Charles Morrow in the lobby of Toronto's King Edward Hotel resulted in Morrow offering to sell LaBine an abandoned warehouse he owned in Port Hope, Ontario. LaBine arranged for Eldorado to buy the empty building for nine thousand shares of stock, then trading at $2.00 per share. (Later in the month the stock rose to $8.10. Morrow was delighted.)

LaBine's first concentrate went by river to the railhead. Thereafter, the company decided to ship the ore by air. Leigh Brintnell's Mackenzie Air Service was awarded the contract. Brintnell had first spotted the strange-coloured outcropping from the air on his way back to Edmonton from Aklavik. Marking the location on his map, he mentioned it to LaBine. Without Brintnell's generous guidance, LaBine would never have found his Eldorado.

Brintnell, like Doc Oaks, was an unusual combination of pilot, businessman and entrepreneur, equally at home with Eskimos in his parka and mukluks or in a pin-striped suit wooing Wall Street bankers. He obtained considerable financial assistance from Tony Fokker, the famous Dutch designer of German fighter aircraft during the First World War, aircraft against which Leigh Brintnell had fought. After the war, when Tony Fokker established an aviation business in the United States, Brintnell financed two Fokker Super Universals through Fokker and opened bush operations out of Edmonton and Fort McMurray.

Brintnell hired Marlowe Kennedy, Matt Berry and Stan McMillan as the company's chief pilots. They flew fresh vegetables and supplies into the various mining camps that were springing up along the shores of Great Bear Lake. So rapidly did the business grow that the company was forced to add another aircraft, a Bellanca Cargo Cruiser, dubbed the *Eldorado Radium Silver Express*. McMillan said the Bellanca was one of the ugliest but most efficient bush aircraft of its period. Because of its speed and short take-off characteristics it was the preferred machine for ferrying injured miners out of the camps for medical attention.

In addition to being an astute businessmen, Brintnell was also a superb pilot with incredible physical stamina. In 1932 he moved forty-five tons of vitally needed equipment from Fort Norman to various Echo Bay mining camps in only eleven days, managing to beat the spring breakup of ice by a matter of hours. The Bellanca made regular trips to Echo Bay and brought out $20,000 worth of radium concentrates on each load. In time local prospectors began calling the ungainly-looking aircraft Leigh's Radium Ship.

Downed flyers and air searches for them were always good copy for national papers.

Canada's Governor General, Lord Tweedsmuir (author John Buchan), holding hat and cane, with (l to r) Leigh Stevenson, Harry Hayter, Marlow Kennedy, Wop May, Grant McConachie peering over Tweedsmuir's shoulder, Stan McMillan, Harry Winnie, Chief Justice Harvey, Ted Field, North Sawle, Con Farrell and Jimmy Bell, 1935. (City of Edmonton Archives, 89)

Below: Ford Tri-motor. (Canadian Aviation Museum, 11517)

Right: Dubbed the Leigh Radium Ship, the Eldorado Radium Express took off from the mine site at Port Radium on the shore of Great Bear Lake on 19 March, 1935, carrying the first radium-ore concentrate to the railhead at Fort McMurray. Stan McMillan and Leigh Brintnell flew the inaugural run. (City of Edmonton Archives, 88)

Readers could participate vicariously in the tragedy, drama, hope and suspense. Man's struggle against the elements of nature was something to which every human being could relate. Searches crossed national boundaries. When US flyers Carl Ben Eielsen and Earl Borland were lost in an Alaskan blizzard, Canadian Pat Reid joined the search. In aviation's pioneer days any call for assistance often meant the difference between life and death. Long winter flights tested the skills and experience of every flyer. Pilots had to be prepared for any emergency. A down-filled sleeping bag thick enough for survival at -40° and at least a ten-day supply of food were standard equipment for every person on board. Pilots refused to carry passengers who were not properly equipped.

If a plane was forced down, the rule of thumb was to remain with the aircraft. To attract the attention of searchers, pilot and passengers would tramp out the word "help" in the snow. Those forced down in more remote areas realized they had little chance of being found and faced an agonizing choice: to stay with the aircraft or strike out for the nearest camp, trading post or settlement. The decision depended upon the weather, the distance to the nearest camp,

the pilot's physical stamina and the number of passengers he was leaving behind who might perish without the necessary bush sense. Those who struck out on their own left a note with the aircraft telling rescuers the direction taken and their date of departure.

Most bush pilots have been forced down for one reason or another, and nearly all have had to rescue others. Matt Berry typified the sort of courage and determination needed to save the lives of downed flyers. During his first year as a bush pilot with Northern Aerial Minerals Exploration, he learned that two prospectors had left

their camp in the Barrens at Baker Lake for the Chesterfield Inlet trading post. They were lost in a blizzard, and hope for their survival appeared slim. Berry happened to be the first pilot to arrive at Baker Lake in the snowstorm. For a week he flew through the storm searching for the missing men. "I had no licence to be flying in that weather, and I had no licence to get through," he admitted. One of the prospectors made it to the post at Chesterfield Inlet. The other froze to death. Sadly, the lone survivor lived only to have both his frozen legs amputated. The north could be a cruel mistress.

Later that winter Berry flew a prospector hauling a load of dynamite to remote Bornite Lake in the Barrens, where they were to meet a second plane. They landed, but howling winds threatened to blow the aircraft away. Berry kept the engine running and quickly buried planks in the snow to use as anchors. He attached tie-down ropes to the Fokker's wing struts. It was not enough. Gusts continually lifted the plane off the ice then dropped it hard on its skis. Berry and his passenger worked in a frenzy, hacking holes in the ice under each wing then threading ropes through the resulting ice bridges to secure the aircraft. By the time they finished, their wrists and hands were badly frostbitten. For protection they built igloos, but the wind was so strong that blowing snow filtered through the cracks and danced around the interior like dust devils. For three days they huddled in their primitive shelters until finally the wind died, whereupon Berry unloaded the dynamite and headed for home.

On another occasion, after a bumpy take-off from Fort Smith, Berry looked out the side window of the cockpit and saw that one of his skis had broken at the pedestal and was hanging by its bungee shock cords. Fred Hodgins, Berry's mechanic, was aghast when, with a broad grin, Berry pointed out the damaged ski. Hodgins sat in silence all the way to Fort McMurray, wondering uncomfortably how Berry proposed to land. Berry made a low pass over the settlement to indicate his trouble. By the time he swung the Fokker around to a final approach, a number of people had gathered at the airstrip. Skillfully, he brought the aircraft down lightly on one ski. As the speed dropped the broken pedestal dug into the snow, swinging the aircraft into a

Junkers Ju52 at Gold Pines, Ontario, loading equipment destined for Argosy Gold Mines, 1938. (Public Archives of Canada, PA 88712)

Fairchild FC2W2 of Northern Airways on Mount Hubbard Glacier, Yukon, 1935. (Public Archives of Canada, C 57656)

gentle ground loop amid an explosion of powdered snow.

On a trip from Coppermine, at the Arctic Ocean, to Cambridge Bay, Berry was forced to land in a blizzard with his windshield frosted. On his final approach he opened the side window and poked his head out into the slipstream so he could see to land. He got the aircraft down in one piece, but an ice rock ripped off the undercarriage and badly damaged the machine. A few days later, Stan McMillan arrived to rescue the uninjured Berry. (Berry's main complaint was the monotonous diet of seal to which he had been subjected.)

Later, while flying along the Arctic coast, Berry rescued several marooned missionaries whose schooner had been trapped in ice. Bishop Peter Falaize, two priests and three Eskimo children had trekked inland from the stricken vessel, *Our Lady of Lourdes,* to the mission at Hornaday River, where Berry picked them up at a landing site marked out with coal sacks. On the return flight, Berry noticed a downed plane in a slough north of Fort Smith. He landed to investigate and rescued bush pilot Gil MacLaren. Like most pilots who flew in the north Matt Berry was gifted with an incredible sense of direction, a sort of a navigational sixth sense. Berry's ability to pinpoint a destination over great distances in bad weather without radio or navigational aids was uncanny. He once flew two miners, injured in an accident at Great Bear Lake, five hundred miles through a raging blizzard to reach a doctor. He touched down at the front door of the hospital in Fort Resolution.

There is a fatalistic acceptance by every

Above: Fairchild Super 71 at Longueuil, Quebec, 1935. (Public Archives of Canada, PA 70856)

Below: Wreckage of deHavilland 60 Moth, south of Nakina, Ontario, 12 August, 1936. (Public Archives of Canada, C 33000)

Bush pilot Matt Berry (l) and engineer Frank Hartley (r) stand in front of the loading door of a Canadian Airways Fairchild. Hartley was one of the "black gang" of astonishing aircraft engineers who could keep an aircraft operational under all conditions. (Provincial Archives of Alberta, 66.122/116)

pilot that sooner or later he or she will be involved in an accident. The question is not "if and when" but "how badly and where?" Berry's turn came during the test flight of a Fokker at an Edmonton air show: the aircraft burst into flames shortly after take-off. Rescuers pulled Berry and the airport manger, Jimmy Bell, from the blazing wreck before it exploded. One man, Charles Hodgins, died in the accident. Berry suffered third-degree burns, various internal injuries and several broken bones. No one believed he would fly again. However, after several months in hospital, he limped into Mackenzie Airways and asked for his old job back. The company management suggested gently that perhaps he should consider alternative employment. Berry was adamant.

He went to see his friend Punch Dickins at Canadian Airways. A sympathetic Dickins hired him on the condition that he take a refresher course at his old RCAF training school in Camp Borden, Ontario. Berry agreed and the RCAF accepted Dickins's recommendation to let him fly. It turned out to be a happy occasion for everyone. In spite of some lingering pain from his injuries, Berry had no difficulty in completing the prescribed refresher course and returned to full flying duties.

Fairchild Super 71 being loaded at Longueuil, Quebec, 1934. (Public Archives of Canada, C 33408)

Before long the RCAF asked Berry to help them with a problem. Flight Lieutenant Sheldon Coleman and Leading Aircraftsman Joe Forety were long overdue in an RCAF Fairchild 71. They had been on a photographic survey mission from Hunger Lake to Fort Reliance. The flyers had gone down in an area close to freeze-up with only a week's supply of rations and no firearms. Swiftly, the air force mounted a six-plane search for the missing men. Three weeks passed with no sign of the downed aircraft. Air force officials turned to the private sector for help. Aircraft from Mackenzie Air Service and Canadian Airways joined the search. When the savage northern weather turned violent, Arctic expert Matt Berry was called

in to help. Berry and Frank Hartley took off for Fort Reliance from Cooking Lake in a Fairchild 71, carrying an extra set of pontoons rigged to their aircraft to repair the crippled RCAF machine.

After systematically combing a huge area along Coleman's flight path, an air force pilot sighted Coleman's gasoline drums at Lac de Gras and landed. A note left by Coleman stated that they had half an hour of fuel left and would fly south until they ran out of gas. A local trapper provided the next clue: he told Berry that he'd seen an aircraft flying northwest and that it had not returned. Berry reasoned that Coleman had flown much farther than he had estimated. The weather cleared briefly. Berry flew northwest to Point Lake, on the fringe of the northern tree line. It was open country covered by stunted bush. Flying low along the edge of the lake, he sighted a tent, then the mising aircraft. Coleman and Forety lit a smoke signal and eagerly awaited their rescuers as Berry taxied to the beach.

"What are you fellows hiding out for?" Berry shouted as he jumped ashore and shook hands. Both survivors were famished. Berry discouraged them from eating solid food and instead gave them plenty of hot milk. To keep from freezing, the downed airmen had made a crude stove from a gasoline drum, then foraged for wood several miles from the campsite. As a supplement to what remained of the chocolate and rolled oats from their ten-day food supply, they had eaten wild berries. A confused US newspaper reporter wrote a vivid description of their weeks of hardship, describing enthusiastically how the men had been saved only by eating "Matt Berries." Berry said his years of wilderness flying helped him find the downed airmen in only four days.

Berry supported the idea of commercial air routes over the pole, arguing that these were the shortest distances to Europe and Asia. He added: "Of course, at the present time these routes may seem a little dangerous, as there are such large areas in which a plane could be lost. But the country is excellent for flying and with proper bases, adequately equipped machines, and availability of rescue parties, there is no reason that an intercontinental air service could not

DeHavilland Giant Moth of the Ontario Provincial Air Service. (Public Archives of Canada, PA 120013)

Survivors Flight Lieutenant Sheldon W. Coleman (l) and Leading Aircraftsman J.S. Forety (c) with rescuer bush pilot Matt Berry (r) at Point Lake, Northwest Territories, September 1936. (Provincial Archives of Manitoba, 2491)

be operated with as much safety and regularity as a railroad." The routes were set up less than thirty years later.

The Great Bear Lake Rush lasted only two seasons then died in the freeze-up of 1933, leaving two small producing mines. Attention turned to Yellowknife, on the shores of Great Slave Lake, where gold had been found. Gordon Latham, who had taught school in Edmonton, was one of the prospectors drawn to Yellowknife's gold rush. Before heading north he arranged to have himself appointed the Canadian Airways agent for Yellowknife. During his off-duty hours he managed to stake a number of claims, which he sold later to Pioneer Gold of Vancouver. He invested his earnings in an aircraft, which he used to carry supplies to local prospectors. Latham also operated Yellowknife's first hotel, the Corona Inn, which sounded far more impressive

than it was. The wooden-framed and canvas-roofed structure became the preferred gathering place for gold prospectors. Its large central room served as a dining hall by day and a dormitory by night. When Con Farrell delivered the first airmail to Yellowknife, the bags were lugged to the Corona Inn for sorting. Mail call was after supper.

Pilots who worked this area operated a remarkable air service, unmatched anywhere in the world. Winston Norman, a reporter with the *Northern Miner*, jotted notes during a trip he took with Mackenzie Air Service pilot Al Brown:

At Fort McMurray (l to r), Frank Wedbourne, Guy Rocke and Wop May load the mail sled for delivery to trappers and prospectors in outlying areas. (Provincial Archives of Alberta, 22)

Arrived at Yellowknife dock with sleeping bag at 9:30 A.M. as instructed by pilot Al Brown. Aircraft is a Fairchild. We have a canoe lashed to the starboard pontoon bearing the Royal Coat of Arms with Canadian Post Office printed on the side of the fuselage. Plane loaded with supplies, luggage, parcels, fresh groceries. Took off from Yellowknife Bay. Made five short stops delivering mail and dynamite caps. Dropped in at lake where 25 men are working on mining exploration site. Brown taxied to a small log dock and unloaded mail sacks, several bags of fresh vegetables, and canned food. Collected receipts and wrote down new orders. Next stop Cito Lake where pilot delivered a radio aerial and package of tobacco, taking order for socks and long underwear. Great care on take-off to avoid a number of rocky outcroppings. Pilot delivered canoe at next stop where two prospectors complained about bears breaking into camp and raiding their food cache. 11:00 A.M. Took off, much lighter without canoe. Put down near trenching operation where Al handed over mail and checked receipts. One prospector had bear cub which sniffed about the camp for something to eat. At next lake a prospector provided lunch of fried sausages, jam, bread and tea. Prospector complained his boots did not fit and placed order for larger size. Hungry bulldog blackflies particularly annoying. At next camp we picked up message for geologist in Yellowknife, reminding him that his report was due in Toronto by the following week. Al is also a Commissioner of Oaths and signed mining document for prospector. Next stop Al asked to take a bear skin back to Yellowknife because it had been eaten by maggots.

As they lifted off Brown turned to Norman with a smile. "Being a taxidermist as well as a messenger boy is just part of this job," he explained. At the end of the day they had recorded twenty-six landings and take-offs and had serviced fifty isolated prospectors.

For Brown it had been a typical day's work. To the men in the isolated camps Brown represented the vital link for supplies, security and news from the outside world.

In 1935 Noorduyn Aircraft of Montreal, Quebec, developed Canada's first bush aircraft, the Norseman. It was capable of operating on floats, skis or wheels and carried up to ten people. The rugged, single-engine Norseman became the choice of pilots and bush operators across the country because of it was dependable and easy to maintain. By the time production ceased after the Second World War, Norseman aircraft were being used by the RCAF, the RCMP, provincial and state governments, the US Army Air Corps and commercial operators around the world.

Junkers on skis carrying two canoes. (Public Archives of Canada, PA 88688)

Above: G.H. Finland and his deHavilland "Hornet Moth" at Prince Albert, Saskatchewan, 1940. (Public Archives of Canada, PA 101498)

Below: Noorduyn Norseman IV of Canadian Pacific Airlines on the Saskatchewan River, 1939. (Public Archives of Canada, C 87965)

Boeing A213 "Totem" flying-boat of Canadian Airways, Vancouver. (Public Archives of Canada, C 87003)

Pilot-engineer Joseph Pierre Romeo Vachon managed Quebec Air Limited, a subsidiary of Canadian Airways. In 1937 he was already a legend among the Québecois. After he left Laurentide Air Service Ltd. Vachon was hired by Canadian Transcontinental Airways. His early dream of uniting the string of isolated French-Canadian communities along the north shore of the St. Lawrence River finally became a reality. During the ferry flight from New York to Murray Bay, Quebec, in the new aircraft to be used for the proposed service, he parachuted a sack of mail onto the Quebec City airport. It was the first aerial mail drop in Canada. North shore mail-delivery service commenced on Christmas Day, 1927. During a ten-hour trip, Vachon, the "flying postmaster," completed mail drops over every north shore community.

A year later he was contracted to fly mail between the mainland and Anticosti Island, in the Gulf of the St. Lawrence, and the nine Magdalen Islands. For eleven suc-cessive winters he delivered the mail from Quebec City to thirty-one communities on the north and south shores of the St. Lawrence River. So impressive was his reputation as an all-weather pilot that the Saunders Roe Company of England asked him to fly its giant hydroplane, *Saro Cloud*, in the Mon-treal-to-Vancouver air race of 1931.

Vachon was awarded the McKee Tro-phy in 1937 to honour his pioneering efforts in establishing airmail service in eastern Quebec and in organizing the radio and weather reporting stations throughout the same area. At the age of forty, he joined Trans-Canada Air Lines. He was its oldest pilot.

Radio communications became an indispen-sable part of the growth and safety of northern aviation. Mackenzie Air Service and the Royal Canadian Corps of Signals pioneered a radio network. Leigh Brintnell opened a radio station in Yellowknife, so that remote outposts could call in for unscheduled service and emergency supplies. As his business grew Brintnell bought one of the early Norseman, and in 1937 he hired more pilots. Archie McMullen, Marlowe Kennedy, North Sawle, Pat McPhee and Robert Randall joined Mackenzie Air Service in the mid-1930s.

A steady stream of bush aircraft carrying prospectors, engineers and miners began filling the skies above the northern mining areas. Most of the miners were unemployed farmers or young jobless men looking for adventure. Most had never been underground. Eldorado's radium mines at Great Bear Lake became the richest and most productive of their type in the world, far surpassing operations in the Congo. The Belgian monopoly had been broken. By the late 1930s, Eldorado's Radium City operation was producing seventy tons of ore a day, enough to produce one sixth of a gram of radium.

Passenger and freight costs from Fort McMurray to Aklavik by air were $2.50 a pound in the 1930s — $95.00 in today's monetary terms. Passengers were jammed in

Canadian Airways McKee Trophy Winners, 1937. (Provincial Archives of Alberta, BL200)

Right: Leigh and Carolyn Brintnell on a summer trip to Aklavik. (Private Collection)

Below: WCA deHavilland DH 84 "Dragon" at Gold Pines, Ontario, 1938. (Public Archives of Canada, PA 88929)

Trucking radium concentrate to the railway station from a Mackenzie Air Services Bellanca Air Cruiser at Fort McMurray. (Provincial Archives of Alberta, A5863)

without seats or belts, next to mining machinery and crates of groceries. They developed what became known as "the Fokker stoop." At times, travellers were sprawled face down on top of the cargo, their backsides resting cold and uncomfortable against the cabin ceiling.

Tony Earnshaw, one of Brintnell's engineers at Mackenzie Air Service, pioneered airborne wireless telegraphy. Mackenzie was the first Canadian commercial air carrier to have such a system. Earnshaw set up a station network from the company's base in Edmonton to the Beaufort Sea. Canadian Airways adopted a similar wireless communication system, which kept their Edmonton head office in touch with stations at Fort McMurray, Aklavik and Coppermine. Earnshaw's radio and instrumentation were primitive. The high-frequency vacuum-tube radio on board was capable of transmitting Morse signals over considerable distances, but voice communications between aircraft and ground bases were rarely possible, even when flying directly overhead.

Competition between the country's two major bush operations, Canadian Airways and Mackenzie Air Service, remained fierce as the two companies struggled to expand. Then, out of the blue, a new company appeared on the scene headed by Grant McConachie, a brash young man with a magnetic smile. He called his company United Air Transport. McConachie opened business in 1933 on a shoestring with two second-hand Fokkers, a few employees and the determination to become the biggest and the best in the country. He elbowed his way into business by accepting cargoes that the other two companies turned down — primarily fish and fresh vegetables. Years later, when he was president of giant Canadian Pacific Airlines, McConachie delighted in recalling his start. "I used to sell fruit and vegetables right out of the plane. Oranges were fifty cents each."

Above: Christmas greeting card from pilots of Canadian Airways Limited. Many of the company's pilots had become household names across Canada. (City of Edmonton Archives, A81-26))

Opposite page: Radio operator Henry Roth outside the Canadian Airways office at Cameron Bay on Great Bear Lake. (Provincial Archives of Manitoba, 1638)

Above: Canadian Airways base camp set up at Kasba Lake by Z.L. Leigh to ferry prospecting parties from Stony Rapids to Windy Lake, 1934. (Z.L. Leigh Collection)

Right: Pilot W.E. Catton heating the oil for his aircraft at God's Lake, Manitoba, on New Year's Day, 1935. This operation was rarely photographed as the oil was usually carried indoors. (Provincial Archives of Manitoba, 1471)

McConachie needed a mail contract to guarantee a steady cash flow. Finally, after much persuasion, he enticed the post office into examining his operation. Wedging postal inspector Walter Hale between crates of lettuce and apples, Grant taxied slowly from the shore on Cooking Lake. He noticed the aircraft seemed a bit sluggish, and the controls stiff. When McConachie looked back to give Hale an encouraging smile, he saw to his horror that water was seeping into the cabin. A mechanic had left the caps off the pontoons — something McConachie should have checked for himself before leaving the dock. The Fokker's tail was under water. "I poured on all the power I had and took the plane across the lake to Small Island and beached it to keep from

Salvaging Mackenzie Air Services Bellanca, which hit a crack in the ice on Lake Athabasca and sank. (Provincial Archives of Alberta, 66.122/32a)

sinking," McConachie admitted sheepishly afterwards. In spite of the near disaster, Hale became a good friend and McConachie got his mail contract.

McConachie's wide smile and persuasive powers would have made him a first-class politician, although he was not always successful in getting his point across. An Indian band scheduled for transfer by air to a remote region refused to board his aircraft unless their chief agreed. The chief refused to sanction the trip. Flying was unnatural for everyone but the birds, the chief explained. McConachie suggested: "You never see a

Above: WACO of Wings Ltd. at San Antonio Mine, Bissett, Manitoba, August 1936. (Public Archives of Canada, PA 14874)

Opposite page: Taking off at LaBine Point, Great Bear Lake, Northwest Territories, 1935. (Provincial Archives of Alberta, 79.128)

bird fall. An aircraft can do lots of things birds can't do. They can fly upside down, fly through clouds, and at night, as well as in the day." Certain that he had won the argument, McConachie awaited the chief's decision. The chief pursed his lips thoughtfully and nodded. "I go if you can land on a twig."

Cautiously, McConachie increased his fleet of small aircraft. He introduced the Ford Tri-motor to the north. On one of the first trips in his new "Tin Goose" were two trappers and eight heavyweight Malamute sleigh dogs. As the Ford's three motors accelerated on take-off, the dogs panicked. One bit through its leash and scrambled to

the rear of the plane, where it stood, snapping and snarling, among the wires and pulleys that operated the rudder and elevators. The other dogs tore loose and joined their enraged mate, where a first-class dog-fight erupted. The trappers ran aft to separate the dogs.

McConachie had just lifted the machine off the ice and was skimming the trees on his climb out, when he felt a sudden shift in the aircraft's centre of gravity. The plane's nose rose involuntarily, and the airspeed dropped until the aircraft was close to stalling. McConachie crammed all three engine throttles forward to hold the ma-

chine in the air and yelled to his partner, George Simmons, to run aft and investigate. Simmons grabbed the two trappers and dragged them to the cockpit. With four men up front to counteract the weight in the tail, the nose dropped. For the rest of the trip the four shaken men remained squeezed into the cockpit listening to the howling dogs. When they landed the howling stopped. Grant switched off the motor and switched on his smile. He turned to the others. "Now, wasn't that exciting?"

Shut out from the highly profitable Northwest Territories by the big companies, McConachie opened new routes from Edmonton to Dawson Creek, British Columbia, and to Whitehorse in the Yukon. More mail contracts followed. He recognized the ad-

vantage of operating year-round while his competitors closed down their operations during freeeze-up and break-up. McConachie reasoned that if he had landing strips constructed then all his aircraft could operate year round. Eliminating aircraft downtime during spring and winter change-overs to wheels and skis meant more flying, more payloads and more profit. He renamed his company Yukon Southern Air Transport. The new name had a nice ring to it. He began talking wishfully of developing his air service to fly beyond Whitehorse, to Alaska, then Asia, and finally around the world. Other aviation operators considered young Grant McConachie quite mad.

In spite of newer and better aircraft and im-

Opposite page: Grant McConachie. (Canadian Airlines, F-62)

Below: Grant McConachie's United Air Transport was the first to introduce the Tri-motor to the north. (City of Edmonton Archives, 34)

Above: Boeing B1-E flying-boats teamed with Department of Fishery patrol boats to control illegal fishing and smugglers, 1935. (Provincial Archives of Manitoba, 47)

Below: Bellanca 66-70 Air Cruiser of Mackenzie Air Service Ltd., Eldorado, Northwest Territories, 26 July, 1935. (Public Archives of Canada, PA 14882)

Grant McConachie (r) helps repair a broken ski, 1934. (Public Archives of Canada, C 61902)

proved technology, nothing could replace the skill and ingenuity of the bush pilot. During a landing one day on Woman Lake, one of Leigh Brintnell's pontoons broke through the ice. The strut twisted and the wing tip hit the ice, cracking an aileron. Brintnell scrambled from the partially submerged aircraft, then spent the night in a small mining community. Next morning Brintnell and the miners set planks across the ice. They chopped a channel through the ice so they could pull the plane to the bank. The miners thought Brintnell should salvage the engine and scrap the aircraft. Instead, he started repairs.

First he emptied the ice from the punc-tured float and straightened the twisted strut. Next, he stitched together the torn fabric and repaired the aileron. He tied a small birch tree in position to support the damaged strut. There was ice in the wings but no practical way to get it out without causing more damage. Brintnell decided to try a lopsided take-off. He heated some rocks and stacked them around the engine cylinders and intake manifold to warm the motor. With the engine running smoothly and with the help of the miners, Brintnell taxied his wounded machine slowly to the open water. Holding the control column hard over to the left, he opened the throttles and braced himself against the side of the cockpit. The ice-laden aircraft staggered onto the step, then gradually eased into the sky. With the control column gripped firmly in both hands, Brintnell managed to hold the wings straight and level for the trip back to Hudson. He arrived half frozen and so numb with fatigue that he had to be lifted out of the cockpit.

In a similar incident, Grant McCon-achie broke the tubular strut on his Fokker during a rough landing at a remote lake. Fortunately, help was available at an Indian settlement close by. The Indians invited him to share their meal of muskrat stew. McConachie accepted. "But when I looked in the pot and saw the skull of the poor muskrat staring back at me I lost my appetite." One of the Indians helped him repair the aircraft. They cut a small tree trunk and fitted it inside the broken strut, then wrapped it tightly with strips of wet caribou hide. The

Below: Barkley-Grow "Yukon Prince" of Yukon Southern Air Transport Ltd. (Public Archives of Canada, PA 124181)

Opposite page: Junkers W34 of Canadian Airways Ltd., 1936. (Public Archives of Canada, PA 23184)

leather dried and shrank and McConachie continued his flight.

Northern cargoes were sometimes unusual. Con Farrell carried two piglets in his Junkers from Fort McMurray to Great Bear Lake. The combination of rough air outside and mid-summer heat inside the cabin made the piglets airsick. As Farrell taxied downwind at Fort Rae, an intermediate stop *en route*, he smelled the sick pigs. His stomach churned. He got on the radio. Other operators gleefully announced his cargo of "two sick passengers" to other radio stations along the way. When Farrell arrived at Cameron Bay, he was met at the dock by a group of miners, holding their noses, and the local doctor, who had been informed that there were two seriously sick passengers on board who needed prompt medical attention. The pigs were delivered to a local restaurant for breeding. The female died soon after the trip north; her porker partner ended up as a weekend "special" on the menu.

Later that summer, Farrell moved a crate of baby chicks by air to Hay River. After a delay at Fort Resolution, he decided to check the live cargo in his baggage compartment. The chicks appeared to be in trouble: they were squeezed together in the stifling heat, their tiny beaks gasping for air. Farrell lugged the crate onto the dock, intending to cool the birds off with a drink of water. As he kneeled to scoop up some water, he knocked the crate of chicks into the lake. He jumped into the water and pulled the drowning birds to safety. Carefully, he lay the tiny, limp bodies out on the warm dock planking, separating the living from the dead. He dried the surviving chicks before they caught a chill, gently rubbing them back to consciousness. Amazingly, most of the chicks survived and were delivered to Hay River.

Tom Lamb in his Stinson, July 1935. (Jack Lamb Collection)

Herd of caribou scatter in the Barrenlands at the sound of an aircraft engine, 1934. (Z.L. Leigh Collection)

Tom Lamb got involved in the flying business because of an accident. Lamb owned and operated a successful trading and transportation company, hauling whitefish by sled from Moose Lake, Manitoba, to Cormorant. There, the cargo was loaded into freight cars of the Hudson Bay rail line for the trip to market. In 1932, while crossing Cormorant Lake on a winter road, his tractor train of sleds hit a soft spot on the ice and started sinking. Lamb abandoned the tractor hastily and signalled a passing aircraft for help. Seeing the half-submerged tractor train, his rescuer suggested that Lamb consider flying his fish to the railhead. Lamb considered the idea carefully. The following year, after taking flying lessons, he bought a Stinson aircraft and opened for business.

Lamb's sons learned to fly and joined the company making Lambair the only aviation enterprise in the world piloted by a father and six sons. Over the next three decades "The Flying Lambs" transported trappers, fishermen and prospectors to the isolated communities of northern Manitoba and the Northwest Territories. The Lambs relied on initiative and ingenuity to get the job done. While ferrying freight, Lamb learned that his friend, Dick McDole, a trapper, had died of a heart attack at Sickle Lake. Tom went to pick up the body. When he found that McDole's frozen corpse wouldn't fit in the Stinson, Lamb used an axe to crack the legs below the knee so the body would fit in the storage bay.

During a routine landing on Redsucker Lake, Dennis Lamb's aircraft struck a submerged reef, tearing the bottom of one pontoon. Without some method of draining the water from the flooded compartments the younger Lamb couldn't take off. He walked to the Hudson's Bay Company store and bought ten empty five-gallon cans with airtight stoppers. After removing the top plates from the waterlogged pontoon, he stuffed the cans into the flooded compartments. After forcing out the water Dennis screwed the top plates back in position and took off.

Tom Lamb's most challenging assignment was to transport fifty pairs of beavers to the Tierra del Fuego region of southern Argentina where the government hoped to develop a fur industry. After bringing the animals safely to their destination, he stayed to find a suitable habitat for their survival before flying home. Argentina and Chile

161

Explorers Air Transport
bush pilot Z.L. Leigh (r)
with Fokker Standard at
Fort Rae, Northwest
Territories, 1933. (Z.L.
Leigh Collection)

were subsequently able to develop a thriving export market for beaver pelts. When Tom Lamb coined the slogan "Don't ask me where we fly — tell us where you want to go," he meant it.

Most commercial flying activity in Canada throughout the 1930s was centred in Edmonton. By the mid-1930s, more than thirteen thousand tons of air freight had passed through Edmonton — more than the combined total of air freight carried by planes in France, Germany, England and the United States. Until the late 1930s, Canadian aviation development had been almost entirely the work of private entrepreneurs and the RCAF. Then, in 1937, the government decided to create the country's first publicly owned airline, Trans-Canada Airlines, or TCA, as it came to be known. The company began operations with two Lockheed 10 pas-senger aircraft and a Boeing biplane for mail delivery. The Boeing was also used for survey on the new routes taken over from Canadian Airways. Bush pilot Zebulon Lewis Leigh became TCA's first pilot employee.

Z.L. Leigh was one of a new breed of pilots. They were too young to have served overseas in the Great War. They learned to fly from the instructors and survivors who made it home. Z.L. Leigh (his initials became the meteorological abbreviation for freezing rain) was already an elderly twenty-three in 1929 when he learned to fly in Lethbridge, Alberta. He became a flying instructor and barnstormer, then landed a

Z.L. Leigh in cockpit of Maritime and Newfoundland Airways Fokker, Sydney, Nova Scotia, 1931. (Z.L. Leigh Collection)

job as a Fokker pilot in a small east-coast company with a big name: Maritime and Newfoundland Airways. It operated out of Sydney, Nova Scotia, and flew across the water to Newfoundland. Business was slow. As the Depression deepened, it became slower. When the company went broke in 1931, Leigh joined the RCAF for a training term at Camp Borden, where he took blind-flying and air-navigation courses.

A year later he was back in Sydney as chief pilot for Explorers Air Transport. He piloted a Fokker Standard Universal to Edmonton and began flying into the Northwest Territories. The Depression closed this operation, too, in 1933. Leigh shrugged his shoulders and took a job as chief flying instructor at the Flying Club in Brandon, Manitoba.

When the word went out that Canadian Airways was expanding its operations and looking for experienced bush pilots, Leigh packed his bags and headed to Edmonton. For the next two years he worked in the Barrens and the Northwest Territories, flying out of Fort McMurray with bush veterans May, Dickins, Gilbert, Farrell and McMullen. But unlike them, Leigh felt comfortable flying aircraft on instruments, "blind flying", as it was called. Except for

Opposite page: Marion Orr, Canada's most famous female pilot, with her Fairchild 24C in Toronto, 1936. (Public Archives of Canada, PA 125925)

Below: Fairchild 82 of Dominion Skyways Ltd. on slush ice at Rouyn, Quebec, 1936. (Public Archives of Canada, C 65204)

WCA Junkers W34 flying over Nation Lakes country, 60 miles north of Fort St. James, British Columbia, 1938. (Public Archives of Canada, PA 88951)

basic engine instruments, compass and airspeed indicators, aircraft instrumentation had been non-existent when the older pilots had learned to fly "by the seat of their pants." A new age of precision instrument flying and air navigation had arrived.

On New Year's Day, 1936, Canadian Airways sent Leigh to the Boeing School of Aeronautics in Oakland, California, to take its complete airline course on instrument, night flying and air navigation, in preparation for the government's new trans-Canada air service. When he returned home he was presented with a specially equipped Laird instrument biplane and sent off across the country to teach airmail pilots flying with Canadian Airways the fundamentals of instrument flying. Then Leigh returned to bush flying, operating out of Sioux Lookout and Red Lake, Ontario, and Prince Albert, Saskatchewan. He joined Trans-Canada Airlines in 1937. From then on he flew in a white shirt and blue tie, and wore a uniform with four gold rings on the sleeves. His days as a bush pilot were over. He was only thirty-one.

Three years later, when Germany marched into Poland and the world was again plunged into global war, airline captain Leigh resigned from TCA to become Flight Lieutenant Leigh of the RCAF. He was posted to Dartmouth, Nova Scotia, flying Hudson bombers on anti-submarine and convoy patrols.

The Second World War

On 10 September, 1939, Canada declared war on Germany. Nine days later the first hastily assembled convoy sailed for England. That convoy opened an oceanic "bridge" of ships carrying men, equipment and supplies to the beleaguered British Isles.

In the early months of the war, a lethargic Canadian government decided to employ the RCAF for "home defence" purposes only. In disgust many young Canadians sailed for England and enlisted in the RAF. Stunned by the French collapse in 1940, and by the power of the German Luftwaffe, the Canadian government finally realized the disgraceful inadequacy of its own air power.

The spectacular success of the wartime air-crew training program in Toronto in 1916 had not been forgotten by the British. Canada, they decided, with its wide open spaces, freedom from air attack and direct sea route to the United Kingdom, would once again become the air-crew training base for Britain and her allies. The British Commonwealth Air Training Plan was signed in Ottawa on 17 December, 1939, between Canada, Australia, New Zealand and Britain, making Canada what US President Franklin Roosevelt called the "aerodrome of democracy." Bush pilots, civilian flyers, RAF professionals and US "freelance pilots" made up the training cadre. By April 1940, the first schools had opened. Three years later 97 schools with 184 depots and ancillary units were operating across the country. By war's end 3,000 students were graduating each month.

Most of the early bush pilots were too old to be combat instructors for fighter and bomber air-crews. Archie McMullen and Joseph Pierre Romeo Vachon went to work with the Department of Munitions and Supply. McMullen became a test pilot for the aircraft being repaired in the British Commonwealth Air Training Plan. Later, he was assigned to the Consolidated Aircraft Company in San Diego where he flew their multi-engined aircraft and flying-boats. He ended the war in Edmonton, test flying rebuilt combat aircraft. Matt Berry taught navigators at Portage la Prairie, Manitoba. Punch Dickins managed six Air Observer Schools, which ultimately turned out twelve thousand graduates. Dickins also directed aircraft ferry operations to England. Stan McMillan's long-range navigational skills were put to use when he flew anti-submarine patrols between Newfoundland and Nova Scotia. Later, he ferried Catalina flying-boats on a regular run from Bermuda to Scotland. Z.L. Leigh and Marlowe Kennedy organized the RCAF's air transport service and helped to create the air force's Air Transport Instrument and Night Flying School at Pennfield Ridge, New Brunswick.

By war's end, with a training staff of close to 40,000 and using 3,600 aircraft, Canada had trained 131,553 air-crew – an incredible achievement. Even more astonishing, 80 per cent of the graduates were Canadians. Besides operating the training schools, the RCAF provided men and aircraft to fight with the RAF overseas. At the same time the RCAF provided convoy and maritime reconnaissance patrols against German U-boats along the Atlantic seaboard and, later, against Japanese submarines on the Pacific coast.

Grant McConachie's vision of an air bridge assumed a practical significance when the partially completed string of airports he had established on the Yukon

Opposite page: The RCAF enlisted Stan McMillan for his long-range navigational skills to fly Catalina flying-boats on submarine patrols over the Atlantic, 1943. (Public Archives of Canada, C 57950)

Right: Weldy Phipps, 405 (Halifax) Squadron in England, 1943. (W. Phipps Collection)

Opposite page: DeHavilland DH89A "Rapide" of Ginger Coote Airways Ltd., Chilliwack Lake, eighty miles east of Vancouver, British Columbia, 1941. (Public Archives of Canada, PA 89004)

Above: The deHavilland "Tiger Moth" became the basic Elementary Flying Training School aircraft throughout the Second World War. (City of Edmonton Archives, 51)

Southern Air Transport route to Whitehorse was upgraded by the Department of Transport so the United States could organize airlift operations into Alaska. Blatchford Field, named after Edmonton's aviation-minded mayor of the early 1920s, received a new administration building and magnificent asphalt runways.

The shock from the Japanese attack on Pearl Harbor galvanized the Americans into action. Overseas, enemy aircraft and naval power pushed the Allies back from a series of defensive positions. In the North American capitals of Ottawa and Washington, a Japanese invasion of Alaska and the west coast seemed likely. The government wanted to deploy defence troops. Accordingly, the Americans developed plans to build a fifteen-hundred-mile highway from Edmonton to Fairbanks, Alaska. Grant McConachie

Beechcraft C17R of Mackenzie Air Services. Harry Hayter is standing on the float, 1940. (Public Archives of Canada, C 58323)

acted as adviser to the US officers in command of the undertaking. He made a preliminary low-level survey of the massive road project using a Norseman. American officials were so impressed by this reliable Canadian bush workhorse that they decided to order several hundred of them for the United States Army Air Corps (USAAF). Eventually, 746 were built for the American air force by the Noorduyn Aircraft Company in Montreal.

The chain of airports used by Yukon and Southern was extended by the USAAF to link Alaska with the trans-Siberian airfields, where lend-lease aircraft and supplies were delivered to the Russian air force. More than six thousand aircraft flew from the United States to Edmonton and from Grand Prairie to Laddfield, near Fairbanks, where they were turned over to pilots of the Red Air Force, who flew the planes to Siberia via Nome. The lifeline to the USSR was dangerous for aircraft and flyers alike. The area between Watson Lake and Whitehorse became known as "the Million Dollar Valley" because of the number of aircraft lost there.

Many of the downed young pilots came from the southern United States. They had never experienced such variable weather and incredible cold.

Wop May suggested to senior USAAF officers that a parachute rescue squad be organized. The jumpers would drop into remote areas, locate downed aircraft, then radio their positions to searchers. The Americans embraced the concept wholeheartedly and offered to train Canadians at their parachute jump school in Missoula, Montana. Within a few months the Parachute Rescue Squad went into action. Its members were trained in wilderness survival, first aid and general bush sense. In appreciation of his efforts, Wop May was awarded the US Medal of Freedom. The Red Air Force Commanding General spoke sadly of the young men who died on the route between Great Fall, Montana and Fairbanks, Alaska:

Above: Bell P-39 Aircobras *en route* to Alaska for delivery to the Red Air Force. (City of Edmonton Archives, 50)

Left: The old and the new. A dog team watches as a Bellanca Pacemaker revs up to taxi. (Canadian Airlines, F-68)

"There are graves of those who died among the snows of this route which mean as much to us as those at Smolensk, Stalingrad and Sevastopol. We feel they died fighting beside us."

Number 2 Air Observers School, Edmonton, Alberta. Wop May, general manager, is seated in the centre front. (Public Archives of Canada, C 58015)

To keep the Allied aircraft flying, Leigh Brintnell spearheaded the development of Aircraft Repair Limited. (In the late 1930s, Brintnell had proposed that a small company, Wings Limited, pool its maintenance operations with Mackenzie Air Services.) Aircraft Repair Limited was managed by Harry Hayter, and received its first job from the RAF in 1940, a shipment of Fairey Battles that had been badly mauled by the Luftwaffe during the battle for France. Further shipments arrived after the Battle of Britain. Aircraft Repair's work force expanded. To repair British-built Avro Ansons and Airspeed Oxford aircraft, the shop had to be equipped with a special plywood-forming section. To straighten out the nose cone of a Bell P-39 Aircobra the engineering department designed its own nose jig. Field service units travelled to accidents across the country, making on-the-spot assessments to determine what was salvageable. As his male employees joined the armed forces, Hayter hired large numbers of women to overhaul the planes. Many of the women out-performed the men.

Late in 1941, under the auspices of the giant Canadian Pacific Railways company, the four major western air services, Canadian Airways, Mackenzie Air Service, Yukon Southern Air Transport and Wings Limited, combined to form Canadian Pacific Airlines. In spite of the merger, fierce rivalries remained between the companies. Barney Phillips, one of McConachie's associates, remembered North Sawle landing a Norseman aircraft in Edmonton shortly after the merger. "All the mechanics had 'Canadian Pacific Airlines' on the back of their coveralls by this time, but do you think a former

Mackenzie Airways grease jockey would go out to meet that ex-CAL plane and pilot? Not bloody likely! Hell, if the plane was on fire he wouldn't piss on it."

The rivalry extended into the executive levels. Dickins, May and Brintnell all expected to be tapped for the top job in the new company's western operations. However, to everyone's surprise, it was young Grant McConachie who got the nod to become assistant to the vice-president.

Edmonton remained the hub of northern flying activity throughout the war. In 1943 the city's airport set a world's record of 82,500 take-offs and landings. Airport manager Jimmy Bell described the airport as the key to the north. One day he had to cope with 120 DC3s lined up at one end of the runway ready for take-off, each carrying a cargo of live naval torpedoes. "As the planes fly out to God knows where, I keep thinking of the Viking sailors of old, always exploring as they searched for more trading routes, more knowledge, extending their grasp beyond all horizons. That's what's been going on at this harbour since it first began."

At the end of the war, many of the bush pilot pioneers had reached the top of the corporate ladder. McConachie became president of Canadian Pacific Airlines. Wop

The new shift arrives at Leigh Brintnell's Wings Ltd. Aircraft Repair depot. (City of Edmonton Archives, 47)

May headed the company's western division. McConachie's pioneering dreams were fulfilled when CPA established air links from North America to Asia and South America. Under his direction, CPA also established routes in Europe, India and Australia. McConachie never forgot his roots as a bush pilot. He said: "In terms of transport, the north moved from the Stone Age to the Age of Flight overnight and we are all the better for it."

Joseph Pierre Romeo Vachon returned to Trans-Canada Airlines as a station manager, then became superintendent of maintenance and overhaul, and finally was appointed a regional director. Matt Berry left flying to run as member of parliament for the Yukon and won a seat in the House of Commons. Leigh Brintnell headed a new company, Arctic Airways. Z.L. Leigh won the McKee Trophy in 1946 and rose to become a group captain and the director of operations for the RCAF at air force headquarters in Ottawa during the Korean War. Between revolutions, Harry Hayter managed to pioneer new air routes throughout Central America. Later, he captained Mexico's first transcontinental flight. Stan McMillan helped create Air Surveys Limited. The company completed thousands of square miles of aerial photographic surveys of the Arctic. Punch Dickins held a number of

Right: Cathedral Lake Headwaters on the South Nahanni. (Provincial Archives of Alberta, 79.128)

Opposite page: Edmonton airport manager Jimmy Bell. "I keep thinking of the Vikings and the men of old ... always exploring, trying to further trade and knowledge by extending their grasp beyond all horizons." (City of Edmonton Archives, 57)

Above: Canadian Pacific Airlines Junkers Ju52.
(Canadian Airlines, F-66)

Below: Canadian Pacific Airlines Junkers Ju33.
(Canadian Airlines, F-64)

Left: Loading a horse into a Junkers Ju52 at Beauchese, Lake Manuan, Manitoba, 1941. (Provincial Archives of Manitoba, 1104)

Below: Parking lot and flight line of Ansons at Edmonton airport. (City of Edmonton Archives, 49)

Ansons and Airspeed Oxfords undergoing repair at
Wings Ltd. (City of Edmonton Archives, 52)

M.O.S. R.C.A.F.

executive jobs with CPA, then worked for deHavilland aircraft in Toronto.

Norm Forrester, the ex-boxer and bush pilot, joined Canadian Pacific Airlines. His luck continued to hold. Scheduled to fly a DC3 on 9 September, 1949, from Quebec City to Baie Comeau, Forrester agreed to change places with another pilot who wanted to be with his girl-friend, a crew member. A few hours later the plane crashed near Ste. Anne de Beaupré, killing all twenty-three persons on board. It was the first incident of an intentional mid-air destruction of a passenger aircraft in peacetime by someone on the ground. Passenger Rita Guay had unwittingly carried on board a lethal device given to her by her husband. Painstaking investigation of the aircraft debris produced the vital clues that led to J. Albert Guay's arrest. After a thirteen-day trial Guay was convicted and sentenced to death.

Archie McMullen joined Canadian Pacific Airlines, which, during his absence, had absorbed his old firm, Mackenzie Air Services. Archie's bush experiences were put to use when he became a CPA check pilot for the Edmonton district. Later, he oversaw the flying abilities of pilots ferrying personnel, supplies and building materials to the Distant Early Warning radar bases being constructed along the rim of the Arctic Ocean. He retired in 1963, after a thirty-year career in which he had amassed 22,000 hours as pilot-in-command on thirty-eight different types of planes without injury to a passenger or damage to an aircraft.

Wartime women gas jockeys gassing an Avro Anson at Edmonton airport. (City of Edmonton Archives, 46)

Left: Atlas Aviation
Beaver on balloon tires,
Ellesmere Island, 1964.
(DeBlicquy Collection)

Below: Beechcraft E17B
and deHavilland "Rapide"
seaplanes moored near
Brandon Avenue, Winni-
peg, Manitoba, 1947.
(Public Archives of
Canada, C 52708)

Ansons, Consolidated Canso amphibians and Beechcraft C45s. Hundreds of two- and three-plane bush and charter operations sprang up throughout the north. A few failed. Most succeeded.

Russ Bradley learned to fly during the war. Like thousands of other young men discharged from the RCAF in 1945, he knew only one profession. He decided to put his flying experience to work and opened a training school at Ottawa's Uplands airport. However, it didn't take him long to realize that he could do more if he operated from his own airport, away from the gimlet-eyed government aviation inspectors who infested the nation's capital. He looked around for a surplus air-force hangar in an abandoned wartime airport, and settled finally for the town of Carp, twenty miles west of Ottawa. He bought the empty hangar, leased the airfield and applied for a variety of operating licences: charter, flying school, aerial photography and crop dusting, each of which required special approval by a government-appointed — and very politically minded — Air Transport Board.

A decade later, through perseverance, good management and a lot of luck, Bradley Air Services had seventeen pilots and thirty-five full-time employees. The company's aircraft were as diversified as its activities. Bradley open-cockpit Boeing Stearman sprayers flew each year on the annual "Operation Budworm" forestry-spraying program in the provinces of New Brunswick and Quebec; twin-engine turbo-supercharged Beechcraft were engaged in vertical aerial photography at thirty thousand feet; the same aircraft used magnatometer and scintellometer equipment to perform a variety of low-level aerial surveys. Bradley was willing to try his hand at anything that would make the company a profit and keep his growing fleet of aircraft busy. He flew charters, gave lessons, flew a helicopter, flew into the bush. But had it not been for the imagi-

nation of Welland Phipps, his taciturn chief of operations and vice-president, Bradley might have been remembered as one of many successful post-war aviation entrepreneurs. Instead, he is known as the man who made it economically possible to explore and develop the high Arctic.

Weldy Phipps's sole ambition in life was to be a pilot. Like Russ Bradley, he served in the RCAF. He flew Halifax bombers with 405 Squadron. When the war ended, he found himself unemployed. To stay in the game he decided to try barnstorming, drawing crowds with a parachute bought from one of the war surplus stores that had opened in every town in the country. "It worked like a charm. I made seven jumps in all, packing my own chute after each. I was just starting to enjoy it when along came the chance to start bush flying at Murray Bay, Quebec. So, I began doing something more sensible than leaping out of airplanes." A few years later he joined Bradley Air Services in Carp.

During the late 1940s and early 1950s interest in the Canadian High Arctic intensified. Oil companies, federal agencies, Canadian and American armed forces interested in building radar defences, and the Arctic Institute of North America all wanted to know what was up there. Was it habitable? Defensible? Worth developing for oil and minerals? Worth protecting? The Arctic and Antarctic were the last unexplored frontiers of the world. Since Russia and Canada shared the bulk of the Arctic region public curiosity and political imperative demanded that the empty areas surrounding the North Pole be explored, investigated, catalogued and developed in the name of scientific progress. The first tentative ventures employed large cargo aircraft capable of landing on man-made airstrips. They carried supplies to various base camps to operate during the long summer days when climactic conditions were bearable. Helicopters and light single-engine aircraft were used to

Above: Norseman IV , at Cross Lake, Manitoba.
(Canadian Aviation Museum, 219)

Opposite page: Junkers W34 aircraft wrecked near
Summit Lake, British Columbia, 1948. (Public
Archives of Canada, PA 102416)

monopolies of inefficient aircraft operators.
Yet it wasn't all bad. In the first two decades
after the war, several hundred new airports
were built across the nation, from single-
runway grass or gravel bush strips to modern
and multiple runways at the deserted airports abandoned by the British Commonwealth Air Training Plan. Every town wanted
an airport. Before long many had it.

The federal government launched a
massive aerial survey operation to update
the map of Canada. For the first time, four-
miles-to-the-inch maps of the north were

available, with every lake, creek, settlement
and hilltop accurately depicted. Visual navigation became a breeze for bush pilots.
Radio navigational aids were installed from
coast to coast, crisscrossing the most travelled air routes. The new bush planes built
by deHavilland, Cessna, Piper and Fairchild
were better, stronger, more flexible and
safer to fly. The preferred choice for those
whose ambitions and dreams exceeded their
cash was the modified surplus Second World
War Noorduyn Norsemen, deHavilland
Moths, twin-engined Douglas DC3s, Avro

End of an Era

The Second World War ended. Thousands of young qualified pilots and mechanics were released from the armed forces and went looking for work. Surplus military aircraft were inexpensive, and provided an ideal opportunity for young ambitious flyers who were willing to work long hours for little pay in order to remain in the only profession they loved and understood. Aviation history was repeating itself, only this time the romance had worn a little thin. After seven brutal years of war, people thought aviation and aircraft meant fighters, bullets, bombers, destruction and death. They wanted to forget. Yet the starry-eyed youths — young-old men now — who had fought the battles of the skies over Europe and the Pacific were as determined as their predecessors a quarter of a century earlier. Against all odds and despite every financial or business misfortune, the new bush pilot entrepreneurs rose slowly, like rich cream, to the top of the jug.

But it was tough. New government legislation and operating restrictions tended to stifle competition and support the local

Three Mile Island seaplane base. The two Barkley-Grow aircraft belong to Canadian Pacific Airlines. (Public Archives of Canada, PA 101855)

Weldy Phipps at the Carp, Ontario, air show, 1947.
(W. Phipps Collection)

explore from the base camps. The helicopters could land anywhere but were enormously expensive to ferry north and operate. Fixed-wing aircraft, while less expensive, required prepared landing strips to function. Yet without helicopters and small courier aircraft there could be no swift practical exploration of the region.

During construction of the Distant Early Warning radar, Bradley was awarded several lucrative contracts for his Cessna

180s as courier aircraft, flying between the radar construction sites. But when construction finished, his Cessna business dried up, and helicopters again ruled the Arctic skies for short-haul contract work. Bradley decided he needed an inexpensive sturdy aircraft with a strong undercarriage that

Above: Picking up the Plaisted expedition at the North Pole, April 1968. (W. Phipps Collection)

Below: Weldy Phipps checking over charts at Ward Hunt Island for flight to North Pole, April 1968. (W. Phipps Collection)

Above: Central Northern Airways WACO 6 Custom, 1949. (Canadian Aviation Museum, 207)

Left: Pilot R. Ruse on float of WACO 6 Custom at Lac du Bonnet, Manitoba, 1948. (Canadian Aviation Museum, 327)

Piper J3 Cub 65C at Fort William, Ontario, 1949.
(Public Archives of Canada, C 52745)

could land anywhere — like a helicopter.

Bradley had acquired a local Piper Aircraft agency. He believed that the two-seat Piper PA18 Super Cubs could replace the helicopters. A single PA18 could carry the same load as a helicopter and could operate an entire season in the Arctic for the ferry costs of flying a helicopter into the north. Bradley and Phipps developed a new tandem four-wheel undercarriage for the Super Cubs. Phipps tested the prototype on a three-thousand-mile assessment flight, from Carp, Ontario, to Churchill, Manitoba, then on to Baker Lake, Shepherd Bay, Resolute Bay, Eureka and Alert Bay. He landed and took off on every conceivable terrain. The tandem gear, he decided, was still not the answer for High Arctic flying. He had a better idea: oversized, low-pressure balloon tires that would allow the Cub to land virtu-

ally anywhere a helicopter could land. The Goodyear Tire and Rubber Company in Akron, Ohio, agreed to produce the giant four-ply tires. Bradley's engineers went to work and designed necessary modifications to the PA18's wheel hubs and brake assembly.

The finished product looked grotesque, but it worked. With a tire pressure of only 4/psi the PA18 could land and take off safely at gross weight, rolling softly over obstacles that would normally have caused serious damage to an aircraft equipped with a standard undercarriage. Airborne drag from the enlarged wheels cost only ten miles per hour of airspeed. Elated, Bradley and

Above: Consolidated Canso flying-boat of Queen Charlotte Airlines, which made the first airmail flight from Vancouver to Kitimat, British Columbia, 22 April, 1952. (Public Archives of Canada, PA 124232)

Right: Republic Seabee amphibian. (Public Archives of Canada, PA 102391)

Opposite page: Grumman "Widgeon" of Pacific Western Airlines at Kemano, British Columbia, 1951. (Public Archives of Canada, PA 102376)

Bradley Air Service Arctic pilot with his PA18 and balloon tires. (DeBlicquy Collection)

Phipps promptly equipped a fleet of Super Cubs with their new invention, held a pilot training course, then sent their men and machines off to the Arctic under contract to a variety of grateful customers.

Each Super Cub carried an incredible array of equipment: a full instrument flying panel, a transistorized lightweight high-frequency radio, a second VHF radio, a low-frequency receiver, a three-hundred-foot wind-up trailing aerial, an astrocompass for taking sun shots for navigation. Radio communication *en route* could be established with various Arctic weather stations and with the Bradley Air Services base camp.

Standard survival equipment included a "Sarah" (an emergency locator transmitter),

tool box and spares, high-powered rifle, pup tent, sleeping bag, a small cooking stove that operated on aviation fuel, first-aid kit, flares, fishing gear, a three-week supply of concentrated rations, a hydrogen generator and balloons. Two kites were provided to lift radio aerials into the air. The aircraft's normal fuel load of thirty gallons was increased to sixty by installing a removable tank in the rear seat for ferry flights. An electric pump transferred the additional fuel into the wing tanks as required. The extra fuel gave the Super Cub a nine-hundred-mile range, or nine to ten hours of air time.

Most of the time Bradley's pilots operated from unprepared glacier strips, shale peaks, mud flats and tundra. Upon their arrival in the Arctic, Phipps taught the inexperienced new pilots about the flying hazards: "Always land on high ground; avoid sea ice and landing on river beds, outwashes or banks unless identified as gravel. Always land uphill and into wind but not into cliffs, and approach steeply after making an inspection circuit. Land so that the last part of the roll is on the smoothest part of the ground."

Veteran Arctic pilot Dick deBlicquy cautioned the eager young novices about the phenomena of Superman Syndrome. "It happens in the busy summer months. A young pilot goes north for the first time and becomes seduced by the absence of darkness and believes he can work around the clock. After a few days of virtually non-stop flying he drops from exhaustion and has to be shipped home."

During their second summer, Bradley and Phipps established a base at Resolute for servicing the fleet of Super Cubs that was fanned out across the top of the world. Meanwhile, at Carp, experiments were under way with larger balloon tires installed on deHavilland Beaver and Otter aircraft.

For his contribution to the development of Canadian aviation, Weldy Phipps was awarded the McKee Trophy. Later, Phipps formed his own company, Atlas Aviation, based at Resolute, where he continued bush flying in the high Arctic. He sold the company and retired in 1972. He resides in Bermuda.

Dick deBlicquy still works for Bradley on a reduced schedule. He still enjoys the Arctic's annual silly season, beginning in late February, when daylight reappears after the long, lonely three months of Arctic winter night. "Every new Arctic dawn brings the crazies out from around the world. They want to travel to the North Pole. Most start out from the northern tip of Ellesmere Island. We fly them and their equipment to the site and wish 'em luck."

During the silly season, Bradley Air Services has flown an Australian millionaire and his helicopter, a Japanese man on a trail bike, two men on foot, a diminutive German woman on snow-shoes carrying an oversized backpack, two Frenchmen flying superlite aircraft and other assorted polar visionaries. DeBlicquy shrugs at their determination. "I've been to the Pole, and there's not much there but a lot of ice and snow. Still, I can say I've been there, and I guess that's what these people want to say, too."

Russ Bradley, always a fast, impatient driver, was killed in an auto accident outside Carp in the fall of 1970. The executors of his estate turned the company over to three of Bradley's employees, Ian Kirkonnell, the company accountant, pilot Dick deBlicquy, and John Jamieson, who had no formal business or management training. Jamieson started working with Bradley in 1954, sweeping the hangar floors. In 1970 he became general manager. Nine years later he bought out his partners to become president and sole proprietor of Bradley and its assorted aviation interests. He enjoys being boss and says, "I live with the very pleasant feeling of knowing no one's looking over my shoulder."

Since 1979, under Jamieson's steady hand, the company has expanded steadily. It now has nearly five hundred employees and a huge fleet of training, charter, bush and modern passenger jet aircraft. Its airline division, First Air, provides scheduled Boeing 727 and turboprop service between twenty communities across the Arctic from Greenland to Yellowknife. First Air carries 245,000 passengers and fifty million pounds of cargo each year to such exotic-sounding places as Igloolik, Eureka, Iqaluit, Gjoa Haven, Nanisivik and Nuuk, in Greenland. They also operate a direct flight from Ottawa to Boston. Jamieson is planning to expand that service through to New York.

Would Russ Bradley have been pleased with what happened to his company? Jamieson thinks so. "We can't compete with the two majors in their bidding wars for the smaller carriers. You simply cannot outbid Air Canada and Pacific Western Airlines if they decide to gobble up every feeder operation in the country." Since deregulation of the Canadian airline industry, Bradley's two giant competitors have taken over CP Air, Quebecair, Austin Airways, Norcan, Air BC, Air Ontario and Eastern Provincial Airways. Jamieson has turned down several buy-out proposals because there is no way the new management could assure him that the company would continue to grow in the direction he wants it to take. "I'm a small-town boy from Almonte who believes in the quality of life in small towns. Carp is a small town, population 874. To the best of our ability we're making it a gateway to the north. This is where we started, and this is from where we'll continue to work."

In 1940, at the age of nineteen, Maxwell William Ward joined the RCAF in Edmonton. After four years as an RCAF flying instructor, he went to work with Northern Flights Ltd., flying between Peace River and Yellowknife. A year later he put down his $2,000 savings to finance a deHavilland Fox Moth and founded Polaris Air Services Ltd., a one-man operation ferrying freight, miners, prospectors and trappers about the north. Ward kept the books, maintained the aircraft and flew the open-cockpit biplane. As the business grew he took in another pilot, George Pidgeon, as a partner to form Yellowknife Airways. In 1949 the business failed. Pidgeon left for Montreal to operate a pub, and Ward went to Lethbridge, Alberta, to build houses. He was twenty-eight and had already gone broke once, but he never lost sight of his goal.

Above: Max Ward.
(Public Archives of
Canada, PA 89950)

Opposite page: A very
proud Max Ward standing
on the float of his new
deHavilland Otter, 1953.
(Public Archives of
Canada, C 60892)

Above: Following Wardair's inaugural charter flight, Max Ward joins his flight crew on the ramp behind the passengers. (Public Archives of Canada, C 60889)

Opposite page: Max Ward at the deHavilland factory in Downsview, Ontario, taking delivery of a new twin Otter. (DeHavilland, 46460)

"I used to sit out there in Lethbridge and gaze across the plains to that darned old row of mountains as I pounded shingle nails into a roof and realized that I wanted to see those mountains, to fly over them. Space, distance, everything pulled me back to flying. Then I'd think of the north. That's big country. The biggest we've got. And I'd set to work even harder."

It took him another four years to realize his goal. He returned to Yellowknife and formed Wardair Ltd. with a deHavilland Otter. The new bush plane, with its exceptional load capacity and incredible ability to land and take off from small lakes, was an instant hit with customers. Max and his engineer, John Dapp, put in long hours to make the company a financial success. After several years of fighting Air Canada, CP Air, and the tightly regulated and politically controlled government Air Transport Board

in Ottawa, Ward finally received a licence to operate in the fledgling international air-charter service. He renamed the company Wardair Canada Ltd. and moved its head office to Edmonton.

Using Douglas DC4s and DC6Bs, the new airline began carrying passengers around the world. Ward then moved into the jet age, first with a single Boeing 727, then with Boeing 747 jumbo jets. In 1967 he turned the company public, with himself as its the major shareholder. He was awarded the McKee Trophy in 1973 for his contribution to aviation. Throughout his years of success and expansion Ward insisted modestly, "We're just a bush operation that's

Grumman Mallard aircraft of Pacific Western Airlines, 1956. (Public Archives of Canada, PA 102407)

Group Captain Z.L. Leigh upon retirement from the RCAF in 1957. (Z.L. Leigh Collection)

grown a little bigger."

Sadly, early in 1988, as a result of airline deregulation and stiff competition, Max Ward found that he was unable to compete with giants Air Canada and Pacific Western Airlines (PWA). Wardair International Ltd. and its 4,500 employees were taken over by the PWA consortium headed by Rhys Eaton. The year before, Eaton had absorbed Grant McConachie's Canadian Pacific Airlines and an assortment of feeder airlines scattered around the country. It was the end of an era. Now, only two major airlines operate in Canada and abroad. They are run by accountants and sharp-eyed business administrators who know little and care less about the romance of flying. Ward's shares at the time of sale were worth around $75 million. Not bad for a former bush pilot and sometime Lethbridge roof shingler after thirty-five years of hard work.

Looking back over the seventy years of exploration and development of commercial bush operations I am struck by the fact that it was not the clever lawyers, lightning-brained accountants, sleek bankers or cigar-chomping stock manipulators who created the Canadian aviation industry. The successful pioneers were modestly educated young men of great courage and fierce determination with a love of flying. For men like Wop May, Punch Dickins, Leigh Brintnell, Doc Oaks, Z.L. Leigh, Joseph Pierre Romeo Vachon, Stan McMillan, Grant McConachie, Russ Bradley, Weldy Phipps, John Jamieson, Max Ward and others, it was never the money or fame or even unbridled ambition that drove them, but rather the challenge of the north and the satisfaction of having to meet that challenge day after day … and

Left: Grant McConachie, president of Canadian Pacific Airlines, flying high at the controls, 1962. (Public Archives of Canada, C 61869)

Below: Grant McConachie and the realization of his dreams, 1962. (Public Archives of Canada, C 61894)

Left: Weldy Phipps's twin Otter *Whiskey Whiskey Papa* in High Arctic on wheel skis. (DeBlicquy Collection)

Below: Imperial Oil's Grumman Goose amphibian. (Public Archives of Canada, PA 98740)

Above: Grumman Goose amphibian. Ideal for getting away from it all to a quiet wilderness cabin, 1958. (Canadian Aviation Museum, 6749)

Left: Grumman Mallard amphibian. The choice of "executive" corporate bush pilots, 1958. (Canadian Aviation Museum, 11525)

Opposite page: Canadian Survey Ship *Hudson* in Cambridge Fjord, Baffin Island. (Bedford Institute of Oceanography)

winning.

The era of the entrepreneur bush pilot has ended. In 1987 deHavilland Aircraft announced that it was abandoning production of its twin Otter, the last of its true bush aircraft. No one is likely to fly a $35 million prop jet into the north and take the chance of landing it on a frozen lake or tundra. Today, if an airport is needed it is built. We don't take unnecessary chances with people's lives or with enormously expensive aircraft. No pilot is permitted by law to fly into the vast emptiness of the north without a detailed flight plan, dual radios and navigational equipment, emergency locator beacon, full blind-flying instrumentation, approach plates to every listed airport, plus a detailed knowledge of the weather and at least two landing alternatives to the proposed destination.

Yet there will always be hundreds of small float- and ski-equipped, single-engined aircraft carrying passengers, mail and freight between the isolated communities of the

north. The men and women who fly these modern and ageing aircraft are still bush pilots. But the equipment they use is up-to-date, with every possible radio, instrument and navigational and safety device installed. Risks to pilot, passenger or aircraft are minimal. Somehow the thrill of it all has gone.

Every day and night, airplanes of the world routinely cross the North Pole on flights between Europe and North America. Occasionally, a passenger may pause to look down at the land and lakes below, and perhaps even wonder for a moment about the Canadian pioneers who made these northern air routes possible and who, in the process, turned a vast unknown and empty wilderness into the warm, familiar comfort of a home.

Canadair CL-215 water bomber at work over a Quebec forest fire. (Public Archives of Canada, PA 124225)

Epilogue

THE NORTH

The North's a mighty river rushing onward to the sea;
Thunder in its rapids, quiet eddies 'neath its trees.
It's the beaver slapping water, the grayling leaping high,
Salmon charging homeward to mate and spawn and die.
It's beauty in the morning when misty lakes lie still.
The statue of a bighorn standing guard on top a hill.

The North's a smoking teepee near a clearing by the pines.
A smell of fish and leather where the pemmican is drying.
It's the bite of shoulder packstrap, the muffled snick of pole
To that fly-infested portage for the torture of your soul.
The North is soaring mountains reaching outward to the sun.
It's rivulets, untroubled streams where tumbling waters run.

It's wandering herds of caribou, nomads searching food,
The Arctic fox ayapping and the lonely loon in brood.
It's purple storm clouds gathering in evening's afternoon
To splash the tamarack and pine, pound rivers into spume.
The North's a twilight rainbow from a sun that never sets
On voyageur and trapper and those with no regrets.

It's the honey of the harvest when rivers run awry,
With the ochre hills at twilight trailing cirrus sky.
Gloom that glows and glistens before the setting sun.
One hundred more tomorrows before the night is done.
There's a settling in the forest, bedding down to sleep,
A leaden covered overcast, a stillness in the deep.

Then the drumbeat of the rapids plays the March of Saul
And icy fingers clutch the land as sleet begins to fall.
Echelons of snow geese slash south in curving vees.
A Master Painter's colour splashes through the trees.
The Northern land is slumbering as snow begins to fall
On silent forest, empty hills and frozen waterfall.

The North's a mighty hunter camping far from home.
A cold bewitching mistress to make the senses moan.
A land of deafening silence. A needle-blizzard gale.

The lead dog's bloody paw prints leaping out the trail.
Snapping sleigh dogs snuffing, straining at the trace.
Frozen toes and fingers and a numbness on the face.

In the daylight of the darkness the North is all in white
With the borealis wheeling and a billion stars alight.
An amber lighted window in a Northern trading store
With a cherry-heated Spencer in the centre of the floor.
An eider duffel sleeping bag that traps the body's heat.
A curdling howl of timber wolf when drifting off to sleep.

It's the morning edge of darkness. Smell of bacon frying
In a stunning isolation that can bludgeon the mind.
The evergreens all laden with their snowy arms asag,
Clint and dint of rabbit print, the stately stride of stag.
It's a million miles of solitude, it's everything that's dear.
It's a soaring of the spirit and the heady wine of fear.

Caribou drifting south from the Barrens to the sticks.
Pilots winging North with supplies for winter strips.
The snowy owl unblinking stands watchful in the wood.
The marten, lynx and darting minks go foraging for food.
Then the sun begins its journey far beyond the Arctic rim.
The night-day's frozen slumber pales in dawn, grows thin.

The North is reawakening as it has since time began;
Driblets of melting snow as sunshine warms the land.
The tintinnabulation of a thawing mountain stream,
The soaring jubilation of an eagle's mating scream.
The North's a tiny spotted fawn astride unwieldy legs,
And a rolling rolic bear cub frolic in the forest glades.

Lakes of ice turn punky, dissolve with strumbling crash,
The cathedral halls at waterfalls sparkle as they smash.
The rapid rivers resurrect their rushing to the sea.
Songbirds fly in from south beneath the snow goose vee.
It's a fighting for survival in a land that never scrimps.
It's gravel, pan and sluice-box for gold that rarely glints.

While the suffocating cities are rupturing our world
With a hundred different races and epithets to hurl,
There's a rustiness of reason, a mustiness of cause,
A dustiness of season because men no longer pause.
The North's the only leveller 'twixt man and beast and sod.
It's the rainbow to my heaven and the open road to God.

Canadian Survey Ship *Hudson* passing a 325-foot-high iceberg in Baffin Bay. Since four-fifths of an iceberg is underwater, the size of this monster can only be imagined. (Bedford Institute of Oceanography)

Index

Acadia, 83
Adair, Harry, 44
Aerial Experimental Association (AEA), 9
Aerial Service Company, 32
Aero Club, *See* Edmonton and Northern Alberta Aero Club
Air BC, 200
Air Board, *See* Canadian Air Board
Air Canada, 200, 204-5
Air Observer Schools, 169
Air Ontario, 200
Air Surveys, 183
Air Transport Board, 191, 204
Aircraft Repair, 176
Airspeed Oxford, 176, 179
Aklavik, 82, 98-113, 120-30, 145-7
Alcock, John, 24
Alert Bay, 193
Antarctic, 191
Anticosti Island, 144
Armstrong, George, 21
Arctic, 39, 45, 67, 82, 107-10, 183, 191-9
Arctic Airways, 183
Arctic Institute of North America, 191
Arctic Ocean, 82, 83, 91, 98, 111, 135, 185
Argosy Mines, 134
Assiniboine River, 100
Athabasca, 30, 71, 118, 130
Atlas Aviation, 199
  Beaver, 190
Austin Airways, 200
Avro aircraft,
  Anson, 47, 176, 179, 185, 189-91
  Avian III, 72, 74-9, 100

Baddeck No. 1, 10
Baffin Island, 208, 215
Baie Comeau, 185
Baker, Major Robert F., 85
Baker Lake, 82-91, 133, 195
Balchen, Bernt, 56-8
Baldwin, Casey, 10
Balgonie, 10
Barker, William G., 18, 27
Barley-Grow "Yukon Prince", 158, 187
Barr, Harry, 44

Barrenlands, 47, 71, 82, 133-4, 161, 165
Barrier River, 125
Bathurst Inlet, 87, 91-3
Bay Maud, 87, 91, 93
Beauchese, 181
Beaufort Sea, 147
Becker, Cy, 18, 74, 79
Beechcraft aircraft,
  C17R, 174
  C45, 191
  E17B, 190
Belgian Congo, 130, 145
Bell, Alan, 93
Bell, Alexander Graham, 9
Bell, Jimmy, 15, 131, 137, 177, 183
Bell P-39 Aircobra, 175-6
Bell River, 125
Bellanca aircraft, 66-70, 67, 112, 124-7, 129, 151
  Air Cruiser, 156
  Cargo Cruiser, 131
  Pacemaker, 97, 102, 175
Bennett, R.B., 111
Bernard, Joe, 121
Berry, Matt, 130-3, 140, 169, 183
Bertangles, 17, 18
Beverly Lake, 83, 88
Bishop, William Avery ("Billy"), 16, 18, 27
Bishop-Barker Flying Company, 27, 30
Bissett, 152
Blatchford, Ken, 44
Blatchford Field, 79, 173
Bleriot flying machine, 13
Boadway, Ed, 82, 85
Boeing, William, 24
Boeing aircraft,
  A213 Totem flying-boat, 144
  B1E, 64, 156
  biplane, 163
  C3 seaplane, 24
  flying boat, 101
  727, 204
  747, 204
  Stearman, 191
  turboprop service, 197
Boeing Air Transport, 110
Boeing School of Aeronautics, 167
Borland, Earl, 132
Bornite Lake, 134

Botha, 9
Bouncing Bronco, 47
Bow, Dr. Malcolm, 73,
Bowen, Jack, 44-5, 124-7
Bowness Park, *See* Calgary
Brackley, Major, 24
Bradley, Russ, 191-200, 205
Bradley Air Services, 191-200
Brandon, 165
Bras d'Or, 10
Brinkman, Ralph, 74
Brintnell, Leigh, 67, 88, 98, 107, 130-2, 145-7, 157-8, 176-7, 183, 205
Bristol fighter, 15
British Columbia Horse, 13
British Commonwealth Air Training Plan, 169, 188
Brown, Al, 140-2
Brown, Arthur, 24
Brown, F. Roy, 111
Brown, J. Roy, 91-4
Brown, Roy A, 16-8, 60, 83, 88-91
Brownlee, James, 100
Buchanan, W.J., 71
Burnside River, 93, 94
Byrd, Admiral Richard, 63

CJCA, radio station, 75-7
Cache Lake, 55-9
Calder, Paul, 118-9
Caldwell, Jack, 45, 47-9
Calgary, 11, 24, 27, 45, 47, 67, 71, 73, 79
  Aero Club, 67
  Bowness Park, 27
  Exhibition (1919), 23
  Stampede, 27, 29
Cambridge Bay, 86, 91-3, 135
Cameron Bay, 114, 148, 160
Camp Borden, 15, 42, 44, 54, 137, 165
Camp Petawawa, 10
Canadair CL-215, 211
Canadian Aerodrome Company, 10
Canadian Air Board, 33, 43
Canadian Airways (CAL), 101-2, 105, 118-29, 137-40, 144-50, 153, 163-7, 176
Canadian Corps of Signals, 15
Canadian Expeditionary Force, 15
Canadian Pacific Airlines (CP Air), 147, 176-7, 180-3, 185-7, 200-6
Canadian Pacific Railways, 176
Canadian Transcontinental Airways, 144
Carcross, 8, 102
Cardwell, 13
Caremon Bay, 118
Carp, 191, 195, 199-200

Carter, Constable, 124
Cat River, 71
Catalina flying-boat, 169, 171
Cathedral Lake, 183
Catton, W.E., 150
Caudron fighter, 13
Central Canada Airlines, 49
Cessna, 188, 192
Cheeseman, Silas A., 53, 56-7,
Chesterfield Inlet, 70, 133
Chilliwack Lake, 173
Churchill, 43, 56-7, 62, 70, 82-3, 195
Cito Lake, 141
City of Edmonton, 27, 40
City of Winnipeg, 52
Clarke, Jack, 49
Clarke, Joe, 22, 27, 32
Claxton, Brooke, 18
Clifden, 24
Cold Lake, 52
Coleman, Sheldon, 138, 140
Collishaw, Raymond, 16, 18
Commercial Airways, 67, 100-1, 105, 108
Congressional Medal of Honor (U.S.), 18
Consolidated Aircraft Company, 169
Consolidated Canso, 191, 197
Cooking Lake, 138, 151
Coppermine, 120, 135, 147
Coppermine River, 91
Cormorant Lake, 161
Corona Inn, 140
Coronation Gulf, 91
Cranberry Portage, 60, 88
Cross Lake, 188
Cruickshank, Andy, 88, 91-3, 114-8
Crystal Beach, 24
Curtis, Glenn, 9
Curtiss aircraft,
  H-16, 33
  HS-26, 44
  HS-2L, 32, 33, 43, 49
  JN-4 Canuck Jenny, 21, 22-9, 32, 44
  Lark, 48
  motor, 10
Curtiss-Wright Corporation, 10

Dapp, John, 204
Dartmouth, 32, 167
Dawson City, 98
Dawson Creek, 155
Dayton-Wright FP-2, 42
Dease Point, 84-91
de Blicquy, Richard, 199
Decoux, Fr., 39

de Havilland, 185, 202
  Beaver, 199
  DH 84 Dragon, 146
  DH89A Rapide, 173,190
  83 Fox Moth, 105, 200
  Giant Moth, 139
  Hornet Moth, 143
  Moth, 74, 131, 188
  Otter, 199, 201
  Tiger Moth, 173
  Twin Otter, 202, 207, 210
de Lessys, Count Jacques, 13
Department of Munitions and Supply, 169
Department of Transport, 173
Depression (1930s), 109, 111, 113, 129, 165
Derbyshire, Peter, 22-3, 27, 30-2, 35, 39
Dickens, Clennell Haggerston ("Punch"), 13, 44-5,
  69-82, 91, 98-118, 137, 165, 169, 177, 183, 205
Distant Early Warning radar bases, 185, 192
Distinguished Flying Cross (DFC), 16, 44
Distinguished Service Cross (DSC), 16
Distinguished Service Order (DSO), 16
Dominion Explorers Club, 81, 88
Dominion Explorers (Domex), 69
Douglas, William, 121
Douglas aircraft,
  DC 3, 177, 188
  DC 4, 204
  DC 6B, 204
  DC 7F, 7

Eagle River, 125
Eames, Alexander, 121-7
Earnshaw, Tony, 147
Eastern Provincial Airways, 200
Eaton, Rhys, 205
Eielson, Carl Ben, 132
Echo Bay, 107, 131
Edmonton, 22, 27, 30, 35-6, 41, 44, 47, 59, 67, 69, 73-
  4, 79, 91, 98, 100, 112, 119, 124, 127, 130, 137, 147,
  155, 163, 165, 169, 173, 177, 181, 185, 200, 204
Edmonton and Grand Prairie Aircraft Company, 44
Edmonton and Northern Alberta Aero Club, 74, 79
Edmonton *Bulletin*, 23
Edmonton *Journal*, 23, 26, 75
Eldorado, 156
Eldorado Gold Mines, 107-9
Eldorado Mining and Exploration, 129-31, 145
Ellesmere Island, 190, 199
Elliot, Warner, 63
Ellis, Frank, 24
English Bay, 101
"Eskimo Joe", 85-90
Eureka, 195

Explorers Air Transport, 162, 165
Explorers Club, 83

Fairbanks, Alaska, 173-4
Fairchild aircraft, 81, 82, 88, 98, 137, 141, 188
  FC2W2, 135
  71, 107, 115, 138
  Super 71, 136, 138
Fairey aircraft,
  Battle, 176
  Mark IIIC, 33
Falaize, Bishop Peter, 135
Falkenberg, Carl, 13, 18
Farmen ("the Rumpety"), 15
Farrell, Conway, 15, 67, 114, 118, 120, 131, 140, 160,
  165
Felixstow F3, 33
Field, Ted, 131
Finland, G.H., 143
First Air, 199
First World War pilots, *See* World War I, pilots
Fitzgerald, 71
Fixed-wing aircraft, 192
Flying Club, 165
Fokker, Tony, 130
Fokker Company, 57
  seaplane, 110, 111, 118, 134, 137, 151
  Standard, 67, 162, 163, 165
  Super Universal, 52, 62, 69-71, 81-8, 91-4, 97, 99,
    114, 130
  Tri-motor, 54
  Triplane, 17-8
  Universal monoplane, 8, 53, 56-9, 62, 95, 98, 137, 158
Ford Tri-motor, 132, 152
Forety, Joe, 138, 140
Fort Chipewyan, 120
Fort Churchill, 55
Fort Fitzgerald, 91
Fort Frances, 58
Fort Good Hope, 45
Fort McMurray, 67, 99, 117, 120-4, 130-4, 141, 145-7,
160, 165
Fort McPherson, 121
Fort Norman, 32, 35, 37, 131
  expedition, 35
Fort Providence, 37
Fort Reliance, 120, 138
Fort Rae, 114, 118, 160, 162
Fort Resolution, 99, 114, 135, 150
Fort St. James, 166
Fort Saskatchewan, 41
Fort Simpson, 36, 39, 98, 99
Fort Smith, 124, 134
Fort Vermilion, 72, 73-5, 77-8

Fort Worth, 15
405 Halifax Squadron, 171, 191
Franklin Hotel, 119
Fraser River, 47
Fullerton, Elmer, 36-40

Garlund, Karl, 123-4
General Motors School of Aviation, 42
Gibson, William, 10-1
Gibson aricraft,
  Multiplane, 10
  Twin, 10
Gilbert, Walter E., 13, 48, 61, 109-10, 114, 118-20, 165
Gilbert, Jean, 118-9
Godfrey, Earl, 56
God's Lake, 150
Godsell, Philip, 39
Gold Pines, 51, 64, 95, 134, 146
Golden, 27
Goodwin, Don, 82-5, 94
Goodyear Tire and Rubber Company, 195
Göring, Herman, 18
Gorman, George, 15, 11-7, 18, 30-5, 39-41
Graham, Stuart, 32
Grand Prairie, 44
Grange, Edward, 15
Great Bear Lake, 67, 82, 91, 107-9, 114, 118, 129-35, 140, 145, 148, 152, 160
Great Northern Flying Company, 42
Great Slave Lake, 36, 82, 91, 140
Great Western Airways (GWA), 67
Greene, H.V., See H.V. Greene Aerial Survey Com pany
Greenland, 199
Grumman aircraft,
  Goose, 207, 208
  Mallard, 204, 208
  Widgeon, 197
Guay, Albert, 185
Guay, Rita, 185
Gwan, Major, 24

H.V. Greene Aerial Survey Company, 30
Hale, Walter, 151
Hamman, Dr. Harold, 74, 77-8
Hammell, Jack, 65-6
Hammondsport, 9
Handley-Page bomber, 24
Hartley, Frank, 138-40
Harvey, Chief Justice, 131
Hay River, 36-7
Hayter, Harry, 131, 176, 183

helicopters, 191-2
Herschel Island, 98
Hersey, Earl, 123-7
High River, 47, 74
Hill, William, 36, 39
Hogarth, David, 88
Hollick-Kenyon, Bertie, 13, 88-91, 93
Hornaday River, 135
Horner, Babe, 79
Horner, Vic, 74-9, 97, 98
Hoy, Ernest, 24, 27
Hubbard, Eddie, 24
Hudson, 215
Hudson, 51, 56, 158
Hudson Bay, 57, 70, 98
  rail line, 161
Hudson's Bay Company, 36, 39, 75, 85-8, 121
Hunger Lake, 138
Hunt, Reginald, 9
Hunter, John, 98

Illustrated London News, 13
Imperial Munitions Board, 13
Imperial Oil, 35, 41, 207

Jackfish Island, 83
Japp, Alex, 11
Jamieson, John, 199, 205
Jeppeson, Elrey Borge, 110
Jeppeson Airway Manual, 110
Johnson, Albert, 121-7
Johnson, Eric, 109
Johnson Walter, 39
Junkers aircraft, 142, 160
  F13, 35, 36-40, 41
  Ju 33, 180
  Ju 52, 134, 180, 181
  W34, 101, 102, 158, 166, 188

Kasba Lake, 150
Kelly, Howard Atwood, 130
Kemano, 197
Kennedy, Marlowe, 130-1, 145, 169
Kent Peninsula, 93
King, Alfred, 121-4
King, Harry, 114
King William Island, 110
Kirkonnell, Ian, 199
Kitimat, 197
Kitty Hawk, 9
Knight, Stanley Neil, 120

LaBine, Gilbert, 107-9, 129-31
LaBine Point, 129, 130, 152
La Pierre House, 125
Labrador, 30
Lac de Gras, 138
Lac du Bonnet, 111 194
Lac la Biche, 47
Lac La Ronge, 107
Lac la Tortue, 32, 42
Lacombe, 45
Laddfield, 174
Lake Athabaska, 70-1
Lake Dubawnt, 71
Lake Stuart, 40
Lake Whenton, 71
Lake Winnipeg, 83
Lakeside, 13
Lamb, Dennis, 161
Lamb, Tom, 160-3
Lambair, 161
Lambert, Bill, 74
Latham, Gordon, 140
Laurentide Air Service, 32, 144
Laurentide Pulp and Paper Company, 32-3
Lebeau, Albert, 36
Lefleur, Joe, 74
Leigh, Zebulon Lewis, 118, 162-9, 183, 205
Lethbridge, 24, 27, 163, 200, 204, 205
Liard River, 30, 39
Lilienthal, Otto, 9
Lindburgh, Charles A., 110
Link, Theodore, 35
Little Bear Lake, 39
Little Red River, 73-4, 77
Lockheed, 10
  Vega, 95, 97-8
London Mail, 13
Longley, Graham, 93
Longueuil, 136
Lord Tweedsmuir, 131
Lougheed, Allan, 98

MacAlpine, Charles, 69, 81-94
MacAlpine expeditionary search, 88, 91-4, 95, 114
McCall, Fred, 15, 18, 26-9, 33, 67
McCombie, Robert, 32
McConachie, Grant, 131, 147, 151-5, 158-60, 169, 173-7, 183, 205, 206
McCurdy, J.A.D., 161
McDole, Dick, 161
McDowell, Bert, 122-3
McKee, J. Dalzell, 56
McKee trophy, 56, 110, 144, 145, 183, 199

MacKenzie Air Service, 112, 129, 130, 137-40, 145, 147, 156, 174-6, 185
Mackenzie Mountains, 98
Mackenzie River, 35, 37, 39, 82, 100, 105, 108, 110, 113, 123, 130
MacLaren, Donald, 13, 18, 101
MacLaren, Gil, 135
McLennan, 76
MacLeod, George, 30-1
McMillan, Stan, 82-5, 97, 98, 130-1, 132, 135, 169-71, 183, 205
McMullen, Archie, 101, 109, 113, 118-9, 121, 145, 165, 169, 185
McMullen, Ressa, 119-20
McPhee, Pat, 145
Mad Trapper of Rat River, *See* Albert Johnson
Magdalen Islands, 144
Malcrow Lake, 94
Maritime and Newfoundland Airways, 163, 165
May, Court, 22, 41
May, Violet, 73, 78, 79, 119
May, Wilfred ("Wop"), 13-8, 21-4, 27, 30-5, 41-5, 73-9, 95-100, 121-7, 131, 141, 165, 174-7, 183, 205
May Airlines, 22
May-Gorman Company, 30, 35, 41
Mikkwa River, 73
Military Cross (MC), 16
Millen, Edgar, 121-7
Mills, Harvey, 100
Milne, Alex, 82-5
Minaki Lodge, 49
Minoru Park, 27
Moar, Jack, 104
Moose Lake, 161
Morrow, Anne, 110
Morrow, Charles, 130
Murray Bay, 144, 191
Musk Ox Lake, 93
Muskoka lakes, 30

Nadin, William, 69, 118
Nakina, 136
Narrow River, 56
National Aviation Museum, 40
National Geographic expedition (March 1935), 8
Naval Air Service HS-2L, 33
Nelson River, 70
Newfoundland, 47, 165, 169
Nieuport fighter, 16
Noorduyn Aircraft Company, 174
Norcan, 200
Norman, Winston, 140-2
Norseman, 142, 143, 174, 188

North Pole, 191, 193, 198, 211
Northern Aerial Minerals Exploration, 65, 133
Northern Airways, 135
Northen Flights, 200
Northern Miner, 82, 140
Northern Syndicate, 45
Northold Airport, 15
Northrop, Jack, 98
Northwest Territories, 35, 113, 152, 155, 161, 165
Norway House, 69

Oakes, Sir Harry, 129
Oakland, 110, 167
Oaks, Harold ("Doc"), 15, 48-57, 98, 205
128th Moose Jaw Battalion, 15
Ontario Provincial Air Service (OPAS), 48, 67, 139
Orr, Marion, 165
Ottawa, 183, 191, 199
Our Lady of Lourdes, 135

Pacific Western Airlines (PWA), 197, 200, 204-5
Parachute Rescue Squad, 174
Parmenter, Lewis, 98-9, 110
Parrsboro, 24
Patricia Airways and Exploration Company, 48
Peace River, 30, 36, 39, 72, 73, 75, 77-8, 111, 118, 200
Pearce, Richard, 69, 82
Peel River, 121, 124
Pelly Lake, 88
Pennfield Ridge, 169
Phillips, Barney, 176
Phipps, Weldy, 171, 191-9, 205-7
Pidgeon, George, 200
Pioneer Gold, 140
Piper aircraft, 195
  J3 Cub 7, 188, 195
  PA18 Super Cub, 195, 198
Pitwitonel, 59
Pochon, Marcel, 130
Point Lake, 139
Polaris Air Services, 200
Port Harrison, 115
Port Hope, 130
Port Nelson, 57
Port Radium, 110, 132
Portage la Prairie, 169
Pour la Mérite, 16
Pratt & Whitney, 53
Prince Albert, 94, 105, 143, 167
Prince George, 40
Prince Rupert, 40, 98

Quebec Air, 144, 200

Quebec City, 144, 185
Queen Charlotte Airlines, 197
Queen Maud Gulf, 86

Radium City, 145
Randall, Robert, 145
Rat River, 121-7
RE.8 reconnaissance aircraft, 15
Red Air Force, 174-6
Red Lake, B.C., 48
Red Lake, Ont., 167
Red River, 82, 122, 124
Redsucker Lake, 161
Regina, 71
Reid, Pat, 88, 98, 132
Reilley, Tom, 98-9
Reindeer Lake, 43
Rene, 36-40
Republic Seabee, 197
Resolute Bay, 195, 199
Richardson, James, 49-53, 62-7, 101, 113
Richmond Gulf, 98
Richthofen Flying Circus, 16, 18
Rickenbacker, Eddie, 18
Riddell, Robert, 123-7
Roche, Guy, 141
Ross, Rod, 56-7
Rothesay, 54
Royal Air Force (RAF), 18, 169
Royal Canadian Air Force (RCAF), 7, 43, 113, 137-42,
  163-9, 183, 191, 200
Royal Canadian Mounted Police, 35, 71, 77, 121-7,
  142
Royal Canadian Signals Corps, 123, 145
Royal Flying Corps (RFC), 13, 15, 16
Royal Naval Air Service (RNAS), 16, 17
Ruse, R., 194

St. Albert, 23
Ste-Anne-de-Beaupré, 185
St-Hubert, 60
St. John's, 24, 48
St. Lawrence River, 144
St. Maurice Forestry Protective Association, 32
St. Maurice River Valley, 32
St. Omar, 15, 17
St. Paul, Charles, 107-9
San Antonio Mine, 152
Saskatchewan Government Airways, 94
Saskatchewan River, 143
Saskatoon, 35
Sault Ste. Marie, 43
Saunders Roe Company, 144
Sawle, North, 131, 145, 176

Schiller, Duke, 70
Scott, Stanley, 32
Shelby, 67
Shepherd Bay, 195
Shirley's Bay, 46
Sickle Lake, 161
Siers, Thomas William, 57, 93-4
Sigesmund, Sam, 53
Silver Dart, 9, 11
Sioux Lookout, 44, 48, 56, 63
Sir John Franklin expedition, 110
Slave River, 71
Small Island, 151
Soldier Settlement Board, 44
Solloway, Isaac, 100
Solloway, Mills & Company, 100
Sopwith, Thomas Murdock, 15
Sopwith aircraft,
  Camel, 15, 17
  Snipe, 15
South Saskatchewan River, 10
Spad, 16
Spandau machine gun, 17-8
Spence, Bill, 88, 91, 93-4
Sproule, Walter, 22, 24
S.S. Tutski, 102
Staffel II, 17
Stanley Park, *See* Vancouver
Stark, Bill, 21
Stettler exhibition, 9
Stevenson, Fred, 53, 56-67
Stevenson, Leigh, 131
Stevenson Field, 62
Stinson, Katherine, 21
Stinson, 160-1
Stony Rapids, 71, 150
Stull, E.W., 101
Summit Lake, 188
Sutton, Charles, 88
Sydney, 165

Tailyour-McNeill airport, 41
Taylor, Charles, 35
10 Squadron, 16
The Pas, 8, 62, 94
Thelon River, 71
Thomlinson, Sam, 48
Thompson, George, 85
Thompson, Gerald, 48
Thompson, Tommy, 82
Thorne, Hubert ("Nitchie"), 36
Three Mile Island seaplane base, 187
Timmins, Jules, 129
Toronto, 13, 30, 165, 169
  Globe, 9

Torrie, Horace, 101, 114
Trans Canada trophy, *See* McKee trophy
Trans-Canada Airlines (TCA), 144, 163, 167, 183
Trans-Canada seaplane flight, 56
Tri-motor, 155
Turnbull, W.R., 54
Turner Valley oil fields, 67

Underwood, Elmer, 9
Underwood, George, 9
Underwood, John, 9
Ungava Bay, 65
United Air Lines, 110
United Air Transport, 147, 155
United States Army Air Corps (USAAF), 142
United States Medal of Freedom, 174
Urquhart, Dr., 124, 127

Vachon, Joseph Pierre Romeo, 42-4, 47, 144, 169, 183, 205
Van der Linden, Casey, 109
Vance, Jimmy, 88, 91
Vancouver, 24, 47, 101, 197
  Stanley Park, 101, 104
Vancouver Aerial League of Canada, 27
Vegreville, 41
Vernon Lake, 64
Verville, Joe, 123
Vic, 36, 40, 41
Vickers machine gun, 15, 17
Vickers aircraft,
  Varuna I, 46
  Viking IV, 43, 45, 47
  Vimy biplane, 24
  Vista seaplane, 81
Victoria, 10, 101
Victoria Beach Station, 43
Victoria Cross (VC), 16
Virden, 35
Voice of the Northern Lights, 123
von Richthofen, Baron Manfred 16-8

WACO aircraft, 111, 152
  6 Custom, 194
Waddell, William, 36
Ward, Maxwell William, 200-5
Ward Hunt Island, 193
Wardair, 202-20
Watson Lake, 174
Wedbourne, Frank, 141
Western Canadian Airways (WCA), 51, 53, 55-7, 61-9, 74, 81, 88, 91, 100-1, 110
Wetaskiwin, 23, 25

Whitehorse, 155, 173, 174
Wilson, John, 49
Windy Lake, 150
Wings Limited, 111, 176, 177, 179
Winnie, Harry, 131
Winnipeg, 35, 49, 53, 56, 61, 62, 69, 71, 72, 74, 81, 82,
  93, 98, 99, 190
  Grain Exchange, 53, 88
  Evening Tribune, 53, 93
Woman Lake, 48
World War I, pilots, 13-9
Wright, Orville, 9
Wright, Wilbur, 9
Yellowknife, 63, 129, 140-2, 145, 199, 200, 204
Yellowknife Airways, 200
Yukon, 8, 65, 82, 98, 125-35, 155, 169, 183
Yukon Southern Air Transport, 155, 158, 173, 174,
  176